FACTORY-ORIGINAL
JAGUAR MK1 & MK2

FACTORY-ORIGINAL
JAGUAR MK1 & MK2

Originality guide including 240, 340, S-Type, 420, Daimler V8 & Sovereign

BY NIGEL THORLEY
PHOTOGRAPHY BY SIMON CLAY

Herridge & Sons

Published in 2017 by
Herridge & Sons Ltd
Lower Forda, Shebbear
Beaworthy, Devon EX21 5SY

ISBN 978-1-906133-70-2
Printed in China

CONTENTS

INTRODUCTION AND ACKNOWLEDGMENTS

This early 2.4 litre (Mk 1) owned by Michael Bing represents the very first post-war small chassisless saloon produced by Jaguar. Finished in Pastel Blue (a rarity in a UK registered car), it displays the early full spats over the rear wheels and the cast radiator grille.

A later 1950s model with the 3.4 litre engine, fitted with wire wheels and the more common cut-away rear wheel spats, which was once owned by the period racing driver and motoring journalist Paul Frere. Now the car is in the hands of the Jaguar Heritage Trust.

I have known the family business of Herridge & Sons, and its founder Charles, for many years. Indeed it was Charles who provided my first break into authorship when he contracted me to produce my very first book on Jaguars (*Jaguar Mk 1 & 2: The Complete Companion*), back in the early 1980s. Since then I have written various titles for the Herridge family, not least *Original Jaguar Mk 1 & 2*, which was one of the first publications to follow the principle of compiling information on the original specification, equipment and finishes of specific models of classic cars.

I was therefore pleased to be offered the chance to write another work on this principle, this time incorporating the other Jaguar and Daimler models derived from the original saloons. So this book also deals with the Jaguar S-type and 420 models, plus the Daimler equivalent Sovereign and the Daimler-engined V8 saloons. All the 'compact' Jaguar

The cast radiator grille was only fitted to the early 2.4 litre engine models. Michael Bing's car originated in Midlothian, Scotland and still carries its original registration number.

The Later Mk 1 model with wider radiator grille originally fitted only to the larger engine model, but later standardised for all Mk 1s.

saloons from 1956 through to 1969 are therefore now covered in a single book.

Although the V8-engined cars still used an engine designed and built by the independent Daimler Car Company, everything else about those models and indeed all the cars featured in this book came from Jaguar Cars at their Browns Lane Assembly Plant in Allesley, Coventry. All of them were built alongside other models like the E-type and Mark X, and that factory only ceased car production in 2005 when assembly moved to their Castle Bromwich facility near Birmingham.

All the information covered in this publication is based on known detail and specifications of production models. It was of course not unknown when these cars were new for buyers to specify different or even unique features to be included in their specification, direct from the manufacturer. Such differences from standard cannot be covered here as they are varied and some even unclear. There will have also

This Somerset registered Mk 2 is one of the earliest known to exist and is currently owned by Richard Thompson. It shows the styling changes from 1950s to 1960s models including extra lighting, repositioned auxiliary lights and another different radiator grille.

This picture of the Jaguar Heritage 3.4 litre (Mk 1) emphasises the narrow rear track of these early cars.

been various changes in the design and build of these cars when assembled from CKD (Completely Knocked Down kits) in countries where taxation hindered the importation of complete vehicles, so some local content will have been supplied and fitted. Where possible, details of dates, chassis and engine number changes are included, but again these are notoriously inaccurate because parts bins were emptied of existing components to save money, with the result that many cars were built with what were theoretically old-stock parts.

To complete this book, I have been ably and thankfully assisted by several people who deserve my thanks. Firstly, of course Charles Herridge himself for his faith in me completing the work to his (and I hope the reader's) satisfaction. Credit also to their staff who sub-edited and laid out the copy for the book. Simon Clay completed the vast majority of the photography, in some cases travelling many hundreds of miles around the UK to capture pictures to show the detailed information needed from cars known to be still in original condition or properly restored.

My long time friend and acknowledged expert on the technical issues of classic Jaguars, Ken Jenkins, advised on many specific details from his life-time of knowledge of

Painted in the popular and very attractive Opalescent Silver Blue, this 2.4 litre Mk 2 typifies the standard production model of the period with steel wheels. Owned now by David Rogers, it was once a well known concours contender in club circles.

The epitome of the Mk 2 that everyone can relate to, a car in Carmen Red with chromed wire wheels (although the latter were not that common in period). This car is owned by Tony Springate and has for many years been one of the most photographed examples because of its overall condition and originality.

Tony Springate's Mk 2 displaying distinctive changes compared to the earlier 1950s models, the much larger (by legal necessity) rear light units, wider rear track and the larger rear window.

Cherished by owner Royston Morgan this was the first Daimler derivative of the Jaguar Mk 2, called the 2.5 litre V8. The car is finished in Warwick Grey and unusually for the period on a Daimler, has wire wheels.

Royston Morgan's Daimler shows the subtle differences between this model and the equivalent Jaguar. Apart from obvious badging and the fluted number plate nacelle, the under body valance is different to accommodate the single exhaust pipes either side of the car.

Daimlers were purchased by a more traditional driver, hence most featured steel wheels with hub caps and chrome rimbellishers like this Dark Blue example owned by the Jaguar Heritage Trust. All Daimler derivatives featured a traditional for the marque fluted radiator grille that blended in well with the frontal styling of the Mk 2.

these cars. Although I have previously owned around twenty examples of the models covered here and have built up my own archive of information and experiences, there is no doubt that it would not have been possible to complete a book like this without the support of the Jaguar Heritage Trust, Jaguar Land Rover's official archive of historic information on the Jaguar and Daimler brands.

Finally thanks must be given to those who provided their cars for photography for this book. Without their efforts in keeping such cars in fine original condition, and then making them available for photography, sometimes in less than the best climatic conditions, this book would simply not have been possible. We feature some wonderful examples in a

range of contemporary colour schemes and specifications.

It is extremely rare these days to find original early 1950s Jaguar saloons. Many early cars fell by the wayside as later models took the limelight for many years. It is only in recent years that the early 2.4 and 3.4 litre cars (Mk 1s) have started to come into their own, but even so many examples have only survived as classic saloon car racers. So it was particularly pleasing to find Michael Bing's superb early 2.4 litre car, still with all its original features, and even in one of the rarer colour schemes of the day.

Again referring to the Jaguar Heritage Trust, they have some incredibly important cars in their large collection, including some we have been able to photograph for use

The later incarnation of the Mk 2 with the 2.4 litre engine was called the 240, the obvious change from this angle being the thinner bumper bars. This car was originally registered in Staffordshire and is now part of the Jaguar Heritage Trust collection.

Peter Hammond's 340 with the thinner front bumper design used on all 240/340 models up to the end of production.

The later Daimler models (known as V8-250), like this one owned by Jim Matthews, a well known concours competitor, also featured the thinner bumper bars. Wire wheels were an uncommon option.

in this book. Their 1958 3.4 litre is a prime example, a car that was lovingly refurbished by David Marks of David Marks Garages in Nottingham with support from the Jaguar Enthusiasts' Club. The car was painstakingly refurbished to ensure it kept all its original features including automatic transmission and wire wheels.

The Trust also supplied other vehicles featured in this book, such as the Indigo Blue Daimler 2.5 litre V8 saloon, a lovely unmolested example. They also supplied the 240 saloon as a definitive example of the later interpretations of the company's medium sized saloon, keeping abreast of the competition in a price conscious market.

To cover the longer production run and greater

Jim Matthew's V8 250 displays the later thinner bumper style, compared to the earlier Dark Blue Jaguar Heritage car depicted.

The rear aspect of the later V8-250 model shows the deep rear valance necessary because of the slimmer bumper bar arrangement.

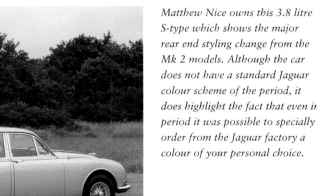

Matthew Nice owns this 3.8 litre S-type which shows the major rear end styling change from the Mk 2 models. Although the car does not have a standard Jaguar colour scheme of the period, it does highlight the fact that even in period it was possible to specially order from the Jaguar factory a colour of your personal choice.

Stylistically the frontal design of the S-type was different to earlier cars with revised lighting and radiator grille.

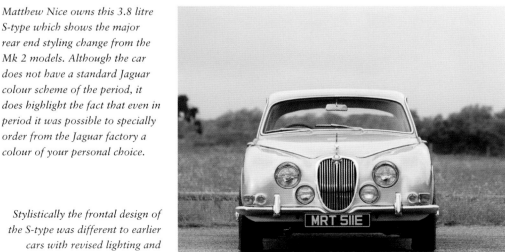

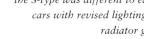

11

New front wings instantly differentiate 420 models from the S-types. Guy Vinyll's car has the rare manual/overdrive transmission and is finished in the popular Opalescent Golden Sand colour.

Quite dramatic changes to the frontal view of the 420 compared to the other models featured in this book. With four headlights, lower, wider grille and the lack of auxiliary lights, the front end echoed the then current Mark X/420G flagship Jaguar saloon range.

numbers of the 1960s Mk 2 range, we have depicted four examples in these pages. The very original 2.4 litre model came from David Rogers, only the second owner of this fine unspoilt example. The 3.4 litre came from Richard Thompson to show representative differences in trim areas between early and later Mk 2 examples, and for the 3.8 litre model, we have to thank Tony Springate who has been the long-time owner and restorer of the magnificent Carmen Red concours example shown here. This is a car that has won many awards over the years and is in the finest condition you are ever likely to find a Mk 2. To finish off the Mk 2 range, we had to incorporate some images of Peter Marshall's very rare 3.8 litre engined 340 example, one of those unusual production cars built with a 3781cc engine to specific owner's requirements.

Returning to the Daimlers, for a contrast in colour scheme and specification we used the 2.5 litre V8 belonging to Royston Morgan and his lovingly cared for but regularly used 1965 example. For the later Daimler (V8-250) model, we have featured another well known concours winner, the Regency Red example belonging to Jim Matthews who has also owned the car for many years, regularly preparing it meticulously with his wife.

The Daimler Sovereign version of the 420 with traditional fluted radiator grille and conventional steel wheels. This car finished in British Racing Green is owned by Patrick Moynihan who still uses the car extensively.

S-types and 420s all benefitted from the same rear end styling treatment, providing owners with a more usable boot area and the fitment of twin fuel tanks. This Daimler Sovereign variant only differs from the Jaguar equivalents by badging on the boot lid and within the rear number plate nacelle.

As well as the Jaguar Heritage S-type, to meet our requirements for an incredibly well restored model, we chose Matthew Nice's 3.8 litre automatic with wire wheels. Although not finished in its original Jaguar exterior paint colour scheme, in all other respects the cars is a perfect example of what was required for this book, and yet another concours winner.

To fulfill the need to cover the 420 models, we have used one totally original and preserved example of the Jaguar model with the quite rare manual-with-overdrive transmission. This car was supplied by Guy Vinall. To complement this we have the Daimler Sovereign automatic from Patrick Moynihan, the Mk 2 Forum Co-ordinator for the Jaguar Enthusiasts' Club.

We thank all these owners for the loan of their magnificent cars, which are a tribute to them and to the heritage of the Jaguar and Daimler brands.

Nigel Thorley
February 2017

A BRIEF HISTORY OF JAGUAR AND DAIMLER

How it all began: the formation of the Swallow Sidecar Company in 1922 manufacturing motorcycle sidecars. (Jaguar Heritage)

This book is not meant to be a definitive history of the two marques, but it is worth mentioning various aspects of that history which relate specifically to the cars it covers. This section therefore provides context and background; later sections then go on to look at the individual types.

The Jaguar Mk 2 saloon has become one of the most iconic of all 1960s sporting saloons and it is a tribute to the original design conceived by William Lyons and his designers that came about with the 2.4 litre saloon in the 1950s. The concept was developed over a total of fifteen years to become a range of cars to suit several pockets and types of owners and which became a benchmark for many other manufacturers. Indeed not only did these models lead to others entering this lucrative market, but they also led to the demise of some manufacturers and their products. The attributes of the range of cars covered in this book were indicative of the company and the foresight of its founder.

As many will already know, Jaguar has its origins in motorcycle sidecar production brought about by two men,

The first cars to carry the Jaguar name were merely Jaguar models within the SS brand, introduced in September of 1935. (Author's archive).

William Lyons and William Walmsley, in Blackpool from 1922. This led to the introduction of their first car, although it was merely a stylish 'Swallow' body on an existing (Austin) chassis. With the help of the Henly Group of distributors, the car was well received and led to other manufacturers' products being similarly bodied, so establishing the Swallow brand.

By 1928, then called the Swallow Sidecar & Coachbuilding Company, the business moved to Foleshill in Coventry to take advantage of all the automobile manufacturing and supply facilities in that area, which was then the hub of the motor industry in the UK. Although the business still concentrated on sidecar production, the company quickly developed via an association with the Standard Motor Company to purchase rolling chassis, and by 1932 Swallow were producing their own cars known as the SS1 (6-cylinder) and SS2 (4-cylinder) models.

SS (Swallow Sports) was now their in-house brand and by the mid-1930s the range of models had grown to eight while sidecars and Austin Swallows also remained in production. There were significant company changes in 1934 with William Lyons taking over sole control of the business and buying out his original partner. The formation of a second company, SS Cars Ltd., signified the forthcoming importance of the car manufacturing side of the business.

The first 'Jaguar' models (then merely a model name as opposed to the brand name which was still SS) were the 1.5 litre and 2.5 litre saloons. Both used engines still supplied by Standard, but significantly re-designed by the renowned engineer Harry Weslake to create the first overhead valve engines to be used by the company. Through the later 1930s the range expanded to include a larger 3.5 litre engined version and hand-built drophead coupé models, plus a low production sports model, the SS100. This latter model created some panache for the company which, of course, was still very small and not particularly well known in the motoring world.

Post-war, the SS insignia was dropped, the cars were given the new brand name of Jaguar, and Jaguar Cars Ltd was formed as a company. During the first couple of years of post-war production, the pre-war designs were built with minor changes, not least the substitution of the Jaguar name.

In 1948 a new but interim saloon called the Mark V was introduced. Although this used the pre-war 6-cylinder engines, it did feature an all-new independent front suspension chassis beneath its traditionally styled but modernised body. This was the first car to be associated with that well known marketing slogan that Jaguar used from then and throughout the range of cars covered in this book - "Grace...Space...and Pace."

Accompanying the saloon was the XK120 sports, which used a shortened version of the new chassis and introduced the legendary XK twin-camshaft 6-cylinder engine that powered all the Jaguars covered in this book and remained in production until 1992. The XK sports developed into the XK140 and then the XK150 whose production ceased in 1961. In 1950 the Mark VII saloon followed the Mark V, using the new chassis, the XK engine and an all-enveloping stylish body to become the flagship of the Jaguar range. It remained in production through various trim and model changes until it was replaced by the Mark X in 1961. The styling of this model certainly influenced that of the cars

featured in this book.

Work commenced on an addition to the Jaguar saloon range in 1952, and this car would eventually be launched in 1955 as the 2.4 litre. The success of this model and its larger engined brother, the 3.4 litre, was instrumental in Jaguar increasing its overall production figures by the end of the 1950s, in William Lyons being knighted for his work in the British motor industry, and in the company achieving its most profitable year of the decade in 1959. Design of the new model took advantage of new technologies, and the cars were somewhat over-engineered by the time they were released in 1955. Well received, the 2.4 litre provided a major stepping stone to greater production numbers and sales, widening Jaguar's customer base.

In the 1960s the Jaguar Group expanded dramatically, and among its acquisitions was the Daimler Motor Company. Daimler was the oldest manufacturer of cars in the UK and had been in financial difficulties for some time. Building its first car in 1896, the company became well known for its bespoke

This period promotional photograph of the 3.4 litre Mk 1 was for the US market. (Jaguar Heritage)

This intriguing press picture produced by Jaguar perhaps emphasises the fact that the Mk 2 was an ideal family car! (Author's archive)

The finishing line at the Browns Lane factory, with Mk 2s coming off the line. (Jaguar Heritage)

coachbuilt models for royalty, dignitaries and celebrities, plus extensive military work during both world wars. The purchase of the company by Jaguar was a major coup that provided valuable additional manufacturing capacity, and a second brand with a reputation for quality cars and even a royal warrant.

As this period began, Jaguar had just introduced its Mk 2, the most successful Jaguar saloon until the introduction of the XJ6 in 1968. Based on the 2.4 and 3.4 litre models, the car was significantly re-designed to rectify criticisms of the earlier cars, and was now offered with a third engine choice, the 3.8 litre XK unit (first seen in the XK150 sports and Mark IX saloon). This inclusion made the 3.8 litre engined Mk 2 the fastest production saloon car in the world at that time.

This was followed by another major success with the introduction in March 1961 of the E-type sports car, followed by the Mark IX replacement (the Mark X) taking on the mantle of the new flagship saloon. This meant that by 1961 Jaguar had completely renewed its entire range!

With the acquisition of Daimler, and to revitalise that business, Jaguar introduced the Mk 2 based Daimler 2.5 litre V8 saloon in 1962. Further expansion in the mid-sized saloon car range included the S-type in 1963, followed by the Jaguar 420 in 1966 which also gave rise to the first badged engineered Daimler, called the Sovereign.

By the time of the XJ6's launch in 1968, the range of saloons was gradually being reduced, in pursuit of a one-model policy. First to go were the S-types, followed by the three Mk 2s in favour of the lesser equipped 240 and 340; the 3.8-litre engine was dropped. The Daimler V8, similarly treated, became the V8-250 and in 1969 all these remaining models were discontinued along with the 420s, leaving the XJ6 saloon to satisfy world demand for both Jaguar and Daimler saloons. So ended the long production run of the models featured in this publication. It was the end of an era.

The launch of the XJ6 coincided with the merger of the Jaguar Group with the British Motor Corporation (BMC) to form British Motor Holdings Ltd, later to be part of the British Leyland (BL) group. Many changes took place during this period including the introduction of the first new Jaguar engine since 1948, the V12 unit, the demise of the E-type in 1974 and the introduction of the XJ-S grand tourer in 1975. Within this time frame Sir William Lyons retired and initially his long time associate FRW 'Lofty' England took over.

The BL period was not one of Jaguar's best, and brought major problems over build quality, employer-employee relations and finance, plus falling demand. Eventually however the business was privatised in the 1980s and then taken over by the Ford Motor Company in 1989. It was sold again to the Indian Tata Group who also bought Land Rover at the time to form Jaguar Land Rover, the business as it is today.

There have been many changes over that period including the re-introduction of a mid-range saloon in 1999, to-recapture the market once held in the 1960s and using the perhaps appropriate S-type name. The car combined a modern approach with a degree of retro styling. This was followed in 2001 by the X-type as an even smaller Jaguar saloon, while the XJ has continued to hold on to the flagship end of the saloon market in various forms. The XJ-S was eventually replaced by a sports car that carried another name from the past – XK – and this was followed by the F-TYPE. Now Jaguar even have their own SUV for the first time, the F-PACE and now even an electric vehicle, the I-PACE.

The medium sized saloon end of the market is now upheld with the XF and XE models, continuing Jaguar's link with the heady days of the models featured in this book, which in their day dominated their sector of the car market.

The classic Jaguar saloons today

With the arrival of the Mk 2 in 1959, the earlier models became known as Mk 1s and were instantly obsolete. Indeed the Mk 2 satisfied all the critics of the previous models with a much brighter, airy interior, improved handling from the wider rear track and extra performance with the availability of the 3.8 litre engine. All this meant that Mk 1 prices plummeted very quickly and remained low for many years. In fact some cars became more valuable as a source of parts for popular and evocative models like the XK sports cars of the period. The Mk 1s remained unloved for years until fairly recently when, due to the popularity of classic saloon racing, there has been a resurgence of interest. These models generally have also become more popular and have increased in value due to the upsurge in classic car prices brought about by the lack of interest rates on investments, making such tangible assets more viable and interesting.

The Mk 2s in contrast have gone through numerous falls and rises in prices and popularity for different reasons. Certainly with the sheer numbers produced and so many cars coming onto the market in the mid to late 1960s, it was inevitable that prices would fall quite severely as depreciation took hold. Then with the introduction of the XJ6 the Mk 2s looked quite dated. The S-types and 420s followed the same pattern but more so because, although they provided an important new marketing approach when new, as used cars they were always eclipsed by the sportier Mk 2.

With the dramatic increases in classic car values in the early 1990s, Mk 2 prices were dragged up accordingly. Such sharp rises inevitably led to a dramatic fall as many people got their fingers burnt, lost interest in the cars and in many cases lost a lot of money as well. This led to a significant decline in interest (and values) of the cars. The Mk 2 and allied models suffered more than some other cars during this period. Fewer came onto the market and even fewer sold at anything like the high prices seen earlier.

It has only been in recent years that significant numbers of cars have come onto the market again, although as usual, buyers have to be cautious about the condition in which they buy them. Values have increased again significantly but not reached their earlier heights, and aspirations for the cars have grown, not least because of their high-profile appearances in TV series such as Inspector Morse and Endeavour.

The Daimlers, S-types and 420s have always been overshadowed by the sportier Mk 2s. This still applies today, although latterly these cars have been finding greater popularity. One reason is that in many cases they can represent better value for money than an equivalent Mk 2, and another is that in some areas they are better cars. For example, both the S-types and 420s offer the much improved independent rear suspension, a larger boot area and – in the case of the latter – the larger and more torquey 4.2 litre engine. In contrast, the small Daimlers offer a very different

An early press photograph of the then new Daimler 2.5 litre V8. Although some Jaguar dealerships were sceptical about the model, it proved to be one of the most popular Daimler private cars ever produced in the whole history of the name. (Jaguar Heritage)

type of driving experience with the ultra-refined V8 engine.

In all cases these models deserve the right to the title of classic saloons. In their day their unrivalled performance, comfort and value for money represented the best in British engineering. Today, compare any aspects of the cars with other classics from many periods, and they still stand the test.

There are areas that need more detailed consideration by anybody who is intending to buy one. While in performance terms the cars remain very capable and are still quick enough to keep up with modern traffic conditions, steering and brakes are products of their day. None of the cars feature items like ABS, and many do not even have power assisted steering. Visibility and safety matters may also cause concern in comparison to modern day airbag-equipped cars. Economy is another issue, as with any of these cars you are unlikely to average more than 25mpg, running on the best 4-star petrol around.

However, hardly anyone is likely to buy such a car for everyday use (unless, as some occasionally do, after modifying them significantly). When driving them is treated as pleasurable and relaxing, they will offer an excellent ownership experience.

The Jaguar Browns Lane Assembly Plant in Allesley, Coventry, was home to the company from the early 1950s through to 2005. It was the place where all the cars featured here were produced. (Author)

THE JAGUAR 2.4 AND 3.4
– AN OVERVIEW

This view of Michael Bing's superbly original 2.4 litre highlights the key features of these early cars with the fully enclosed rear wheel spats and narrow cast radiator grille. Although 15ft in length, the car gives the impression of being even smaller, certainly compared to contemporary equivalent cars like the Ford Zodiac and Vauxhall Cresta!

There was a long gestation period between Jaguar starting the design work on the 2.4 litre model and its launch at the 1955 British Motor Show in London. The curvaceous styling of the new XK120 sports car and Mark VII saloon, along with the new Jaguar XK twin-cam 6-cylinder engine, formed the basis of the new design. Following the early racing and rally successes of the XK, and having established a market for large prestige saloons, William Lyons wanted to capitalise on all this and gain entry into a new market, for a smaller luxury sporting saloon.

Development started in 1952 and Jaguar, looking to the future, opted to build their new model with unitary monocoque (chassisless) construction, a concept still relatively new to the British car industry at the time and a first for Jaguar. The drivetrain followed the then current Jaguar practice, with rear-wheel drive, a four-speed Moss gearbox and, of course the XK engine, this time with a smaller 2483cc capacity.

The 2.4 was not ready for its launch until 1955, when it was offered as a two-model range comprising the Standard saloon and the Special Equipment version. As the name implied, the Standard model was just that. Such already recognised features of SS and Jaguar models as a rev counter and heater were missing, as were lots of other 'trim' items. In reality, although the cheaper Standard model was fully promoted in the early brochures, it never actually went into production. It is doubtful that even pre-production cars were ever assembled, although photographs do appear in the company archive. The Special Equipment model therefore became the norm.

Priced at £1375, the Special Equipment model had a top speed of around 100mph, with the 2.4 litre engine developing 112bhp. Carrying forward Jaguar's quickly established reputation for performance and styling, it was virtually unique among British luxury saloons of the period in what it offered. The 2.4 was built for only three years, from 1956 to 1959, although some of the last production was not registered until early 1960.

The 2.4 was supplemented by a further, more powerful variant from 1957. This was the 3.4, with the 3442cc version of the XK engine from the sports car range. Looking much the same as the 2.4 litre version, it had some trim changes, including a wider radiator grille to improve cooling, and cut-away rear wheel spats. The much improved performance of the 3.4 provided the momentum to drive sales in the USA, where the 2.4 litre had not been that well received. With the introduction of disc brakes shortly afterwards (eventually fitted to all Mk 1s) and the availability of automatic transmission, total sales for both models reached 37,000 despite their short production life.

The smaller Jaguars found favour with many who did not want the gargantuan Mark VII/VIII/IX models, and the cars were highly competitive, bringing Jaguar success in racing and rallying. Nevertheless, the model was criticised on some fronts, particularly the poor front suspension geometry and,

All later Mk 1s were fitted with cut-away rear spats to rationalise the parts bin, and these accentuated the narrow rear track of the 2.4 and 3.4 litre models. Photo by the author.

most important of all, the inferior handling caused by the narrow rear track, which at the time was deemed necessary to accommodate the stylish tapered rear end of the car.

Production of both the 2.4 litre and 3.4 litre models ceased in 1959 to make way for the replacement Mk 2, which rectified any issues that could have been raised about the earlier cars. Since that time all these earlier models have become well known as 'Mk 1s', although Jaguar never actually gave them that designation.

When the larger 3.4 litre engined car was launched in 1957, it attracted the more sporting owners, many of them amateur and professional racing drivers. One result was that wire wheels became common; they suited the style of the car.

THE JAGUAR MK 2 AND DAIMLER V8 – AN OVERVIEW

The differences between the earlier (Mk 1) cars and the Jaguar Mk 2 are many, but the most striking from this angle is the larger glass area, and even the wider rear track is evident.

At the 1959 British Motor Show in London, Jaguar introduced revised versions of their compact saloons with the name of Mk 2. This subsequently led to the unofficial title of Mk 1 being given to the old models. The Mk 2 would form the basis of a whole new range of Jaguars for the early 1960s, and there is no doubt that these models put right all the problems and dislikes associated with the earlier cars.

As well as the 2.4 litre and 3.4 litre engined versions, there was now an even higher performance 3.8 litre model. The 3.8 litre variant of the XK engine was fairly new, having previously been introduced for the XK150 and Mark IX models. Producing 220bhp, it made the Mk 2 the fastest production saloon car in the world at the time, providing a genuine 120mph-plus top speed (in 1959!). All the models featured four-wheel disc brakes, an entirely new interior and a larger

glass area. Although the new models were very similar to the old in overall styling, in reality very few body panels remained unchanged and the addition of more brightwork certainly set the cars off well. All this made the Mk 2 an instant success in that valued North American market, where it became the most prolific Jaguar model exported there during this period.

Prices for the Mk 2 started at a very competitive £1553 in Britain, which put the car very much in contention with the quite sparse competition of the time. Even the most expensive 3.8 litre automatic at £1927 was still incredible value for money for a car providing such performance. The cars were so well equipped that there were not many optional extras you could specify unless you wanted to go racing or rallying – and many early cars were campaigned in this way.

Many changes took place during the Mk 2 production period, as sales through the years continued to prove the suc-

It almost seemed like an afterthought to call the new model the 'Mk 2' and indeed some cars did leave the factory without the badging.

Legal necessity brought about the need for larger rear light units than those used on the Mk 1s. The same considerations affected all other Jaguar models at the time.

cess of the formula. These changes are documented in this book, but the first major upgrade came with the introduction of an all-synchromesh gearbox, replacing the Moss-designed 4-speed three-synchromesh unit that dated back to the early postwar period.

With the introduction of other interesting mid-sized luxury cars in the 1960s like the Triumph and Rover 2000s, and Jaguar's development of its own independent rear suspension leading to the introduction of other Jaguar saloons, it was inevitable that sales would start to decline in due course. So Jaguar started planning for the eventual replacement of the

Mk 2 range. This began with the 3.8 litre model being discontinued in 1967, followed by the 'trimming down' of the other two models, which were renamed 240 and 340 in April that year. This was done to retain the market temporarily at a more attractive price, and indeed brought back prices similar to those at the Mk 2's original introduction in 1959.

Sales continued to slow, so the 340 ceased production in 1968, followed by the last of the range, the 240, in April 1969. A mere 4430 of that particular model had been built, but this does not take away from the impressive production total for all Jaguar Mk 2 (plus the 240 and 340 models) of

Imagine the prestige of arriving home in the 1960s with your new Jaguar 3.8 litre Mk 2, the fastest production saloon of its time, the envy of the neighbourhood!

Despite the Jaguar parentage and style, the Daimler was clearly aimed at a different clientele, the more traditional owner. This was emphasised by its typically more sombre colour schemes, and by the fact that the cars were rarely fitted with wire wheels in their day.

There can be no argument over the superbly balanced styling of the Mk 2, viewed from any angle. Photo by the author.

nearly 91,000 cars. They had been Jaguar's most successful range up to that time.

All this does not account for the Daimler variants. The 2.5 litre V8 was introduced in 1962 as the first entirely new Daimler model for some time, needed to keep the Daimler brand alive after Jaguar's takeover of the company. Despite some concerns among Jaguar folk that it was just a 'crin-kle-cut Jaguar', it was not as 'badge engineered' as the styling might have implied. Edward Turner's magnificent 2.5 litre V8 engine, designed in the pre-Jaguar days to power the SP250 sports car, created an entirely different type of car to drive. It was beautifully smooth and refined, and although it offered little more performance than the 2.4 litre XK-engined Jag-uar, it suited the more conservative market that Daimlers had been Daimler's preserve. Although sales never equalled those of the Jaguar models, they far exceeded expectations and led to the introduction of other Daimler models in the Jaguar range for many years to come. Lyons revitalised the Daimler brand and the name was only dropped from the company range in 2008.

With the rationalisation of the Mk 2 range, the Daimler variant was also treated to a revamp in 1967, with thinner 240/340 type bumper bars and a new name, V8-250. How-ever, the Daimler model retained some of the original luxury features like leather upholstery, which the Jaguars did not. With some minor trim changes the new model was also of-fered with a manual transmission as an option, and remained in production until 1969. Total production of the Daimler variants was under 18,000 examples.

JAGUAR S-TYPE, 420 AND DAIMLER SOVEREIGN – AN OVERVIEW

The centre section of the body is pure Mk 2 although the roof line was altered slightly for the S-type. With the longer boot and revised frontal treatment, plus the availability of only the larger engines, the S-type was aimed at a different market.

In the early 1960s Jaguar Cars were doing very nicely, thank you. The success of their E-type sports and the Mk 2 saloons captivated the market in those areas. The flagship Mark X saloon sold in far smaller numbers on size and price but Jaguar identified a niche in the market for another saloon, fitting nicely between the big Mark X and the sporty Mk 2. This was an attempt to challenge the more modern competition coming on to the market from other manufacturers in this sector, and an opportunity to take advantage of the newer technology Jaguar was using in its other cars.

The S-type was therefore launched as an additional model in 1963 with just two engine sizes, 3.4 and 3.8 litre, each with manual or automatic transmission. At a starting price of £1670 for the 3.4 litre manual, the S-type was only £200 dearer than the equivalent Mk 2 but you got a lot more for your money.

Although the styling was broadly similar at the front, the S-type had a unique treatment, with a re-shaped radiator grille, peaked headlights, and slim bumper bars of a similar style to the Mark X's. The body centre section was virtually the same as the Mk 2's except for the roof and rear screen. The rear however, was significantly modified, akin to the Mark X's, giving the model an entirely new look. This rear end treatment provided enlarged boot accommodation and allowed for the fitment of twin fuel tanks giving a slightly greater fuel capacity.

The major mechanical change came in the rear suspension. Gone was the old leaf-sprung arrangement of the Mk 2, in favour of the independent rear suspension developed for the Mark X and E-type. This was a much more sophisticated arrangement giving improved handling and ride comfort.

In addition, the interior was given a mild make-over, bringing it somewhere between the Mk 2 and Mark X in style and comfort.

The 420 models externally were pure S-type except for the frontal area ahead of the scuttle, yet commanded a higher price with larger 4.2 litre engine and modern styling.

The most significant case of badge engineering after the take-over of Daimler was the Daimler 420 Sovereign. Badging and the addition of a fluted radiator grille were all that separated the car from a Jaguar.

The S-type was in production for a quite short period, from 1963 until 1968 (although some cars were not registered until a year later), by which time Jaguar had decided to scale down its entire saloon model range in readiness for the launch of the XJ6.

It was while the S-type was still in production during 1966 that Jaguar announced yet another new saloon, the 420. This was effectively a hybrid design, taking its cues from both the existing S-type and the Mark X. Very much an interim model, it was obviously produced to maintain sales and interest in the cars until Jaguar could introduce that entirely new saloon that

would be the XJ6.

From the windscreen back, the 420 was all S-type, but the front took on a more modern styling approach echoing the Mark X's, with four headlamps and a shallower radiator grille. Internally the 420 was also a mix, although the majority of the trim matched that of the S-type.

The big change was pretty obvious from the new model name, '420'. The engine fitted was another variant of the 6-cylinder XK unit in 4235cc form, first seen in the 1964 Mark X and E-type models. This time fitted with twin SU carburettors (instead of the three in the other 4.2 litre-engined models), this engine was also the forerunner of the one fitted to the later XJ6. The 420 was available with either manual or automatic transmission.

There was to be another variant of the 420, for Jaguar had also decided to launch it as a Daimler, calling it the Sovereign. For the first time this was effectively a 'badge engineered' car – Daimler in name, but with hardly any difference from its Jaguar 420 equivalent. Indeed, the only changes amounted to the badging and fluted trim. It was never intended to fit Daimler's own V8 engine due to costs and practicalities.

With a starting price of £1930 the 420 was £100 dearer than the equivalent S-type 3.8 litre, cheaper than the larger Mark X, and filled another niche in the market. Jaguar now had a vast range of saloon models from the 2.4 litre Mk 2 through to 4.2 litre Mark X, plus the Daimlers.

By 1969 the last of the smaller saloons, the Daimler Sovereign, had been dropped, shortly after the one-model-policy XJ6 had been launched in September 1968. The total production run of all S-types and 420s amounted to 41,000 cars.

ENGINES

There were only two engine designs fitted to all the cars featured in this publication, the Jaguar XK 6-cylinder and the Daimler V8. We will treat them separately as they are significantly different.

Jaguar XK 6-cylinder twin camshaft engine

This must be the most recognisable engine ever produced by Jaguar, as its design was so well executed and it was fitted to so many models over the years, eventually leaving production only in 1992.

Its design is pretty much the same regardless of capacity. The XK engine capacities used in the cars that this book covers were 2.4 litres, 3.4 litres, 3.8 litres and 4.2 litres. The engine size is cast into the right-hand side of the block. Blocks often carried casting dates on the left-hand side in front of the dipstick hole.

Cylinder block

The cylinder block is made from chrome cast iron. The EN16 manganese molybdenum steel crankshaft runs in seven main bearings with Vandervell steel-backed bearing shells. Alloy split skirt or solid skirt pistons (9:1 compression engines were usually solid skirt) with three rings were fitted to EN16 connecting rods. The 3.4 litre engines had an additional piston ring below the gudgeon pin. The standard compression ratio for all engines was 8:1, but in various applications a higher compression ratio of 9:1 or a lower compression ratio of 7:1 were available according to market or to individual order. The compression ratio of an engine is identified by a '-7, -8 or -9' suffix to the engine number stamped on the cylinder block. The firing order of the cylinders remained the same throughout production at 1,5,3,6,2,4. The numbering started from the rear of the engine and worked forward, following pre-war Standard practice. From April 1959, all engines were fitted with lead indium big end bearings.

The cylinder block incorporated a Bray electric block heater boss (mainly for use in cold climate countries to aid warm-up). From 1960 this boss was moved from the left-hand side to the right-hand side, and although there appears to be some confusion over which blocks actually had a boss after that date, in reality it was all of them.

Sump

2.4 litre engines were initially fitted with an aluminium oil sump pan, although this was changed to a pressed steel version, late in November 1956. In June 1961 sumps were modified to take a larger capacity oil pump. The oil filter housing was still retained by 4 bolts, but was angled down, instead of up as on the early engines. Engine lubrication was by conventional gear pump. The oil filter housing was modified in September 1962 with five fixing bolts instead of four, and a rubber seal was added to the oil pressure release valve and balance valve.

With the introduction of the S-type models a revised aluminium sump pan was fitted to these engines, and in October 1964 it was standardised for all other models. (As an aside, the anti-roll bar thickness was increased from ⅝in to ¾in diameter at the same time as the sump was changed. This made it necessary to fit aluminium spacers between the anti-roll bar mountings and the chassis to give clearance between the anti-roll bar and the sump).

Originally there was no rear main bearing oil seal, just a scroll to act as an oil thrower, and an extension to the rear of

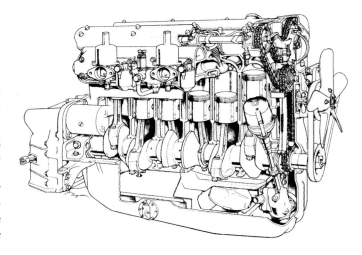

The magnificently engineered Jaguar XK 6-cylinder twin-camshaft engine introduced in 1948 in the XK120 sports car. Later fitted to the Mark VII saloon in 1950, it also powered most other Jaguar models for many years, not least all the cars featured in this publication except for the Daimler V8s. Photo from author's archive collection.

the sump caught the oil. The scroll was machined down on the rear of the crankshaft, and an asbestos rope seal was fitted from October 1961, still using the steel sump. In September 1962 the oil dipstick handles were increased in length on all engines.

Cylinder head

The twin-cam cylinder head was a masterful design with hemispherical combustion chambers and a two-stage timing chain system. Made of aluminium alloy, it weighed in at less than half an equivalent iron head.

A number of different cylinder heads were fitted to these

Cylinder head types

Model	Engine Designation
2.4 litre Mk 1	B
2.4 litre Mk 2	BG onwards
240	7J001 onwards
3.4 litre Mk 1	KE - KF
3.4 litre Mk 2	KG - KH - KJ
340	7J50001 onwards
3.8 litre Mk 2	LA - LB - LC - LE
S-type 3.4 litre	7B
S-type 3.8 litre	7B
420	7F
420 Sovereign	7A

models (see Panel). The A type came directly from the original XK120 and Mark VII models of the early 1950s, but with a revised inlet manifold to match the type of carburettors fitted. This was used on the 2.4 litre engine with 5/16in lift camshafts. The 3.4 litre and 3.8 litre cars always used the B type head, which had better porting, larger exhaust valves, and 45-degree valve seat angles. (The A type head used 30-degree seat angles to improve low speed flexibility). The 240, 340 and early 420 models all used the same straight-port cylinder head. Apart from the 2.4 litre, the other models, including the 240, all had ⅜in lift camshafts. The late 420 and Daimler Sovereign models had the XJ6 type of head with two extra rear waterways. This head was not polished at the front as were the earlier heads, but was left as a rough casting. The cylinder heads are painted in different colours according to their type (again see Panel).

From February 1957 the camshafts were modified, and changes included a hole drilled through the base of each cam into the main oilway to reduce noise.

Other

From August 1964 cast natural colour (silver) engine lifting brackets were fitted to the cylinder heads via the appropriate head studs. This required longer head studs and a longer plug lead conduit.

The front timing chain cover was revised in August 1964, allowing the front seal to be renewed without removing the cover.

Early installation of the XK engine in a compact saloon, in this case the 2.4 litre from the 1950s. The installation is accurate as are the paint finishes. 2.4 litre engines were the only ones fitted with Solex carburettors and the air cleaner/trunking is unique to the 2.4 litre Mk 1 shown here.

Mk 2 2.4 litre engine bay showing the different cylinder head colouring and the unique oil bath air cleaner arrangement for this model.

XK Engine Type Specifics

2.4 litre

With a capacity of 2483cc, this engine was developed specifically for the 1950s 2.4 litre saloon and continued in use until the end of 240 production in 1969, virtually in the same form. It was never fitted to any other models. It is effectively a short-stroke version of the original 3.4 litre engine but with the same bore. The stroke was shortened to 76.5mm from 106mm, and the connecting rod length was reduced at the same time. This made for an engine block that was 3 inches shorter in height, and the whole engine was about 50lb lighter than the larger 3.4 litre unit.

Originally fitted with 5/16in lift camshafts and producing a modest 112bhp at 5750rpm, the 2.4 litre was fitted with a different inlet manifold to suit the Solex carburettors that were used in place of the larger engines' SUs. The camshafts were modified in February 1957 with holes drilled through the base of each cam into the main oilway to reduce tappet noise.

240

For the 240, in 1967, the major change from the Mk 1 and Mk 2 2.4 litre engine was the cylinder head. The B type cylinder head was replaced by a straight-port version, first seen on the XK150 S models and the E-type, followed by the Mark X. The straight-port head differed in that the ports were less curved, having the effect of confining any turbulence to smaller areas of the combustion chamber, which improved efficiency and boosted power output from the Mk 2 2.4's 120bhp to 133bhp at slightly lower revs. Like its predecessors, even this modified variant of the XK 2.4

The straight port cylinder head 2.4 litre engine installed in this 240 now incorporates a conventional air cleaner arrangement. As there was a crossover period some 240s had polished cam covers, and some very late Mk 2s had ribbed cam covers like these.

litre engine was never fitted to any other models.

With the adoption of the straight port cylinder head, the 240 engine moved over to black-painted ribbed camshaft covers, replacing the previous polished alloy covers, and from then on this was the norm for all Jaguar XK engines.

3.4 litre and 340

This engine application (initially in the 3.4 litre Mk 1) came about because of the need for more power in the Mk 1 for the valued North American market. The engine had the usual capacity of 3442cc and was introduced in February 1957 for the Mk 1 as an additional model. It was essentially the same as the engine fitted to the XK140 and Mark VIIM/VIII models, with larger (1¾in inlet and 1⅝in exhaust) valves than these earlier version, but again it needed a revised inlet manifold.

Though taller than the 2.4, it still fitted well into the engine bay and incorporated a standard B type cylinder head, producing a very worthwhile increase in power from the 112bhp of the 2.4 litre to 210bhp. The 3.4 litre engine was later fitted in the Mk 2 and was also used in the S-type.

It was not until February 1961 that the 3.4 litre engine had a tube added to the sump for the dipstick; previously the stick went straight into the casting.

3.4 litre engine in the Mk 1 installation, still using an oil bath air cleaner. All colour schemes are also correct for this model.

This is an example of a very early Mk 2 3.4-litre engine installation, dating from before the middle of 1960. It features the same oil bath air cleaner trunking arrangement as the 3.4 litre Mk 1 models.

3.8 litre

The 3781cc engine was first seen in the Jaguar XK150 and Mark IX models and was a natural choice for the Mk 2, providing more power (220bhp) and torque than the 3.4 litre unit. The 3.8 litre engine was also fitted to the S-type models.

The cylinder head was the B type as fitted to the 3.4 litre, with a chamfered combustion chamber to allow for the larger bore size; this was deleted in late 1962 when the piston crowns were chamfered instead. A new block was designed, increasing the bore from 83mm to 87mm. The 3.8 litre block incorporated dry cylinder liners for the first time. This came about because although the 3.4 litre block could be bored out, the gap between cylinders was narrower and could therefore cause cracks to appear during manufacture or later in high-performance use. The forward three and rear three bores were interconnected with water passages between the two halves.

The increased brake horsepower was achieved at the same 5500rpm as the 3.4 litre engine and the torque figure increased by about 11½% to 240 lb/ft, which was 37 lb/ft more than the 3.4 litre unit.

As with the 3.4 litre engine, from February 1961 a tube was added to the sump for the dipstick; previously the stick went straight into the casting.

The 340 engine, or as in this case a factory fitted 3.8 litre unit, used another new style of air cleaner arrangement. By this time all the cylinder heads were finished in the same silver colour. Notice the later type of ribbed cam cover with the silver cylinder head finish, retaining the engraved filler cap.

The more commonly recognised engine installation in the Mk 2 with 3.4 litre and 3.8 litre engines. This 3.8 litre unit again shows the different cylinder head colouring and now the 'pancake' air cleaner arrangement, common to all of the larger engine models until the introduction of the 240/340 range.

Engine installation in the S-type, in either 3.4 litre or 3.8 litre forms.

The Jaguar 420 engine installation which retained many of the features of the smaller engines as fitted to the S-types but with revised carburetion and manifolding, cooling system, etc. Again there was a crossover between polished and ribbed cam covers and in the case of Daimler Sovereign variants the oil filler cap either featured an engraved 'D' or was left plain as on the Jaguar.

4.2 litre

The 4235cc engine was introduced with the 420 and Sovereign models in 1966 and this was its first application in this form, with twin carburettors and the straight-port cylinder head. It provided better torque and rather more power than the 3.8 Mk 2, as the performance figures show, and was rated at 245bhp (up from 220bhp) with maximum torque of 282 lb ft at 3750rpm. In this form it was only fitted to these two cars before being used in the new XJ6 from 1968.

The new engine configuration necessitated a new cylinder block. The stroke was the same as the 3.8 litre's at 106mm but the bore was increased from 87mm to 92.07mm. To accommodate the larger bores (still linered) in the same size cylinder block, the spacing of the cylinders was altered so that the centres of cylinders 1 and 6 were moved outwards towards the ends of the block. Consequently cylinders 3 and 4 were moved closer together, leaving cylinders 2 and 5 unchanged. There were no water passages between any bores but the opportunity was taken to improve water flow around the cylinders by modifying the water jacketing.

The crankshaft was naturally also new to accommodate the changed bore size, with thicker webs, rearranged balance weights, and a new damper serving to break down the torsional frequency of the crank. Although the connecting rods and pistons were the same as the 3.8, the pistons had a chromium-plated top ring, a tapered second ring and a multi-rail oil control ring.

The later Daimler V8-250 installation shows its revised twin air cleaner mounting.

Daimler 2.5 litre V8 Engine Type Specifics

This engine was one of two specifically designed for the Daimler Motor Company by the well-known designer of motorcycle engines, Edward Turner. Sister to a larger 4.5 litre V8 engine that was fitted to just one model, the Daimler Majestic Major, the 2.5 litre V8 was designed for smaller cars and was used in Daimler's own SP250 sports car. It was also intended for a new medium-size saloon model, but that never came to fruition. After the Jaguar-Daimler merger, the engine continued to be used in the SP250 until that model ceased production in 1964.

The capacity of 2547cc was achieved with a bore and stroke of 76mm x 70mm, and output was 140bhp at 5800rpm. This engine had a 90-degree cast iron block with twin aluminium cylinder heads which were interchangeable. Valves were actuated from a single camshaft mounted in the centre of the block via composite pushrods with a duralumin tubular centre section and case-hardened steel ends to allow for the expansion of the heads.

After the purchase of Daimler, Jaguar prototyped the V8 engine in a Mk 1 bodyshell and found it very refined and an ideal opportunity to continue producing a Daimler model. Hence in 1962 the Daimler 2.5 litre V8 was launched.

Few changes were required to accommodate the much more compact V8 engine into the existing Mk 2 bodyshell. To make it fit, and easy to service, the studs holding down the cylinder heads were replaced by set bolts which aided removal of the heads while the engine was still in the car. The water pump was repositioned centrally on the front face of the block with split outlets for each bank. Belt and pulley arrangements were also changed for this application.

The V8 engine weighed 1cwt (112 lb, 51kg) less than the equivalent Jaguar engine which helped performance compared to the 2.4 litre XK unit.

The engine continued in production through to the V8-250 model, after which production ceased. It was not fitted to any other Jaguar models.

Two engines were designed for Daimler by the famous motorcycle engineer Edward Turner, a large 4.5 litre unit to power the Majestic Major and a smaller 2.5 litre unit intended for the SP250 sports car and a new smaller saloon that never came to fruition. Such was the refinement and good design of the latter that Jaguar decided to install it in a new Daimler after the company takeover. Photo from the author's archive collection.

ENGINE FINISHES

Cylinder heads
SILVER
All 2.4 litre heads, A type (up to the introduction of the B type).All later heads from the introduction of twin-carb 4.2 litre units (420) and including the straight-port head fitted to the 240 and 340, and V8s.
DUCK EGG BLUE
B type 2.4/3.4 litre engines.
MID BLUE (sometimes metallic)
B type 3.8 litre engines.

Cam covers
Polished aluminium cam covers were fitted to all engines up to approximately 1967-68. This includes all Mk 2s and S-types. Polished alloy screw-fit oil filler caps were embossed with the Jaguar name. Head nuts were domed and chromed.
Ribbed covers with black paint were fitted to engines produced after this time, including the 420, Sovereign, 240 and 340. They retained a polished alloy screw-fit oil filler cap but without the Jaguar name, and chromed domed head nuts.
All V8 cylinder heads have polished alloy covers, which are interchangeable.

Auxiliary equipment

Engine support bracketry	silver
Dynamos	black
Alternators	silver
Radiators	black
Gearbox	silver
Coils	silver
Starter motors	black
Sump pans	black painted steel sumps on all but the first 2.4 litres, all 3.4 litre and 3.8 litre models until late 1962
Oil filters	2.4 and 3.4 Mk 1s, original fit Tecalemit brown or black painted; on later cars, filters are metallic green
Plug leads	black
Master cylinders & pipework	silver
Wiper motor	silver and black
Power steering reservoir	black
Power steering pump	black
Inlet manifolds	polished alloy
Exhaust manifolds	black vitreous enamelled (Jaguar XK) silver high-temperature paint (V8)
Heater box & fan	black (Hardura covered on 420 and V8s)
Radiator fans	black metal
Steering box	black
Pipework	fuel lines copper, heater water pipes black, dipstick tube (where applicable) black
Engine mounts	black
Battery connections, support strap, plastic undertray/upper cover (where fitted)	black
Carburettors	polished alloy

Air cleaners

2.4 litre Mk 1	polished alloy top cover to carburettors, black painted circular steel canister, black sloping section leading through inner wing to black oilbath filter
3.4 litre Mk 1	as 2.4 above but reverse heart-shaped polished alloy section from carburettors with oval-shaped black canister
2.4 litre Mk 2	polished alloy top cover to carburettors (as Mk 1), polished alloy elongated circular top section leading to a black painted circular steel air cleaner with forward facing trumpet air intake
3.4 and 3.8 litre Mk 2	reverse heart-shaped polished alloy section from carburettors to large pancake silver-painted air cleaner on top of the engine with two sideways pointing flattened trumpet air intakes
240	same reverse heart-shaped polished alloy section from carburettors to silver-painted oval steel air cleaner with two short inner wing facing trumpet air intakes, mounted across engine
340	as 240 but with longer oval silver-painted air cleaner and a single downward facing trumpet air intake
V8 2.5 litre	polished alloy piping from each carburettor to a single silver-painted circular pan air cleaner on top of engine with two forward-facing trumpet air intakes.
V8 250	two silver-painted metal circular air cleaners mounted directly onto each carburettor at an angle, with a single forward-facing trumpet air intake to each

ADDITIONAL ENGINE BAY FEATURES

Washer bottle system	Mk 1,Trico circular glass reservoir with black metal threaded flat top and black pipework
	Mk 2, Lucas square glass reservoir with black threaded plastic top with black electric motor and connections
	240 and 340, Lucas oval plastic opaque reservoir with black electric motor and connections
Brake fluid reservoir	2.4 and 3.4 Mk 1, black metal with black metal cap
	Mk 2, early cars, silver metal with black plastic cap.
	Mk 2, later cars, opaque plastic with rubber cover to connections and top

ENGINE SPECIFICATION COMPARISON

	2.4 Mk 1	2.4 Mk 2	2.5 V8	V8-250	240
Capacity	2483cc	2483cc	2548cc	2548cc	2483cc
Cylinders	6	6	8	8	6
Carburettors	2 x Solex	2 x Solex	2 x SU	2 x SU	2 x SU
Type	B32-PBI	B32-PBI	HD 6	HD 6	HS 6
Compression ratio	7:1 or 8:1	7:1 or 8:1	8:1	8:1	7:1 or 8:1
Power (bhp)	112	120	140	140	133
At (rpm)	5750	5750	5800	5800	5500
Torque (lb/ft)	140	144	155	155	146
At (rpm)	2000	2000	3600	3600	3700

	3.4 Mk 1	3.4 Mk 2	3.4 S-type	340	3.8 Mk 2
Capacity	3442cc	3442cc	3442cc	3442cc	3781cc
Cylinders	6	6	6	6	6
Carburettors	2 x SU	2 x SU	2 x SU	2 x SU	2 x SU
Type	HD6	HD6	HD6	HD6	HD6
Compression ratio	7:1, 8:1 or 9:1	7:1, 8:1 or 9:1	7:1, 8:1 or 9:1	7:1, 8:1 or 9:1	7:1, 8:1 or 9:1
Power (bhp)	210	210	210	210	220
At (rpm)	5500	5500	5500	5500	5500
Torque (lb/ft)	216	216	216	216	240
At (rpm)	3000	3000	3000	3000	3000

	3.8 S-type	420
Capacity	3781	4235
Cylinders	6	6
Carburettors	2 x SU	2 x SU
Type	HD 6	HD 8
Compression ratio	7:1, 8:1 or 9:1	7:1, 8:1 or 9:1
Power (bhp)	220	245
At (rpm)	5500	5500
Torque (lb/ft)	240	283
At (rpm)	3000	3750

CARBURETTORS AND FUEL SYSTEM

The twin Solex model B32-PB1-5 arrangement as fitted to the 2.4 litre Mk 1 models. These were also used on 2.4 litre Mk 2, albeit with a different air cleaner arrangement. Of silver finish with brass connections, some of the pipework is unique to the Mk 1 model.

There were only two manufacturers of carburettors used on the Jaguars and Daimlers featured in this book. They were Solex and SU.

Solex

The Solex carburettors were model B32-PB1-5 (of the same type as fitted to the Land Rover Series 1 engines). These were of the downdraught type with a natural aluminium (Mazak) finish. They were only ever fitted to the 2.4 litre engines in the Mk 1s and Mk 2s, and were not used on the 240 engines introduced in 1967.

The arrangement was for the twin Solex carburettors to be fitted with an oil bath type of air cleaner and to be mounted on a revised inlet manifold to fit the XK engine; this was the only time such an induction system was used in this engine. The manifold was of the usual cast alloy type, heated by coolant taken from the cylinder head through cast-in passages.

For the air cleaner in the Mk 1 application, air was drawn in through an oil bath gauze reservoir in the nearside (right hand drive) inner wing area. It was then trunked via the black metal cylindrical air silencer mounted on the cylinder head to a horizontally mounted polished aluminium inlet directly on top of the carburettors.

From April 1956 the air correction jets in the Solex carburettors were changed from 160 to 180 and the needle valve from 1.5mm to 2mm. In November the main jets were changed from 115 to 110, and the 25mm choke tube was altered to 24mm. The carburettors always had 110 main jets

This overall view of the Solex carburettor used in the Jaguar 2.4 litre models shows the finish and fitments. Photo courtesy Bob Bate.

and fuel was fed through to them from the 12 gallon petrol tank mounted under the boot floor via an SU (type AUA 57) fuel pump mounted in the inner rear wing area of the boot.

A manual choke starting device was operated by a lever and Bowden cable entering the dashboard via the steel bulkhead and operated by a slide lever near the steering wheel. The arrangement was quite crude but it did provide a degree of enrichment for cold starting and the dashboard-mounted slider looked good!

From September 1956 the Solex carburettors were modified to incorporate a weir in the float chamber.

On the 2.4 litre Mk 2 engines, the only difference was in the main jet size of 105 and the design of the air bath air cleaner arrangement. In this case, air was drawn in through a trumpet air intake facing towards the front of the car and connected to a black metal circular oil reservoir that was bolted to the exhaust manifold and cylinder head. On top of the reservoir, a polished aluminium trunking was bolted at that end and connected to the same alloy intake mounted on top of the carburettors. The oil bath air cleaner arrangement was also used on the very early 3.4 litre and 3.8 litre Mk 2 engines, but was abandoned in April 1960 for the more conventional pancake style air cleaner arrangement mentioned below.

SU

All the other models featured here used carburettors of SU manufacture. The range covered HS6, HD6 and HD8 types, all with a polished aluminium finish. Dashpot tops were initially in brass, but in around 1963 these were changed to black plastic. All cars were fitted with 1.75in diameter carburettors except for those equipped with the HD8 type.

The single application for the HS6 carburettors was for the 240 (2.4 litre) engine when it was fitted with the straight port cylinder head. These carburettors used TL needles (as also used in the 340 model) and still retained a manual choke system like the Solex installation, although the style of the lever mechanism on the dashboard had changed after the Mk 1 cars.

No longer using an oil bath type of air cleaner, the 240 had a much simpler cleaner assembly based on the one used in 340 and 420 models. A silver painted metal canister of oval section was bolted to the cylinder head and had twin air intake trumpets exiting the side facing the nearside (right hand drive cars) inner wing. This connected at the other end to the inverted heart-shaped polished aluminium intake bringing air to the side intakes of the SU carburettors. A replaceable paper element filter was used.

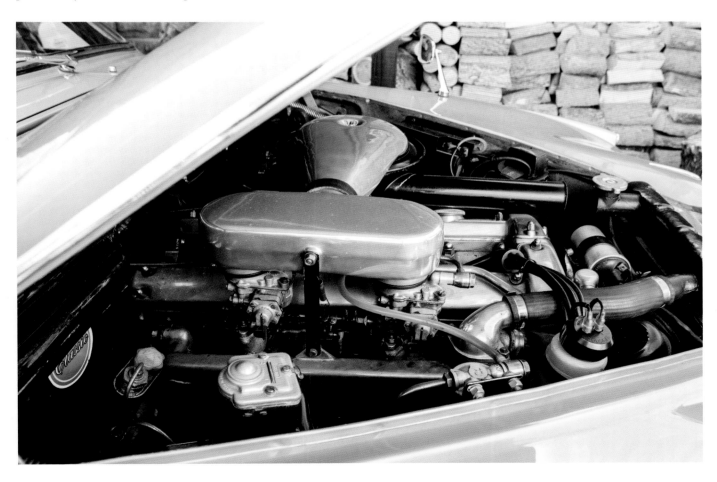

The Mk 2 2.4 litre Solex installation, except in detail very similar to that on the Mk 1 engine.

A close up of the HD6 SU installation for 3.4 litre Mk 1s, 3.4 litre and 3.8 litre Mk 2s. Photo courtesy Bob Bate.

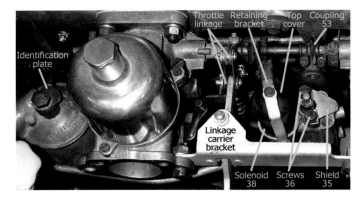

A close up of the HD6 SU installation for 3.4 litre Mk 1s, 3.4 litre and 3.8 litre Mk 2s. Photo courtesy Bob Bate.

The much more common HD6 SU carburettors were fitted to all 3.4 litre and 3.8 litre XK engines with needle sizes according to specification. For earlier Mk 1 and Mk 2 models with an oil bath air cleaner, SC needles were specified. For the later cars with a conventional pancake air filter, C1 needles were specified, in both cases based on 8:1 or 9:1 compression ratio engines. The original fitment from the 3.4 litre Mk 1 required the design of another new inlet manifold with a bolt-on water rail.

The Mk 1 application also involved another air bath air cleaner system, though of a slightly different design to that used on the early 2.4 litre (Mk 1) engines. The cylinder head mounted air silencer, also black painted metal, was of oval section (very similar to that used on the 240) and was mated to the same polished aluminium intake to the carburettors.

This Mk 1 application did not have a manual choke system but instead, like the later 3.4 and 3.8 litre installations, used an SU auxiliary starting carburettor with the rich mixture ducted to points under the inlet manifold, a system that continued in use throughout the production of the Mk 2, S-type, 420, and 340 model ranges. This 'extra' carburettor was fitted between the two main carburettors and drew fuel from the front float chamber, feeding it directly into the inlet manifold when the engine was cold. It was controlled by a thermal switch fitted at the front of the cylinder head. If the starting carburettor was working correctly, an electrical connection cut the switch and stopped the supply of fuel as soon as the engine reached an operating temperature of 30 degrees C.

Many owners complained as the system could be unreliable, and in many cases an electrical switch was mounted on the dashboard so the driver could manually switch off the electrical connection. Others learned that by switching the ignition off and quickly back on again, this would also cut the connection, stopping the excess flow of fuel.

On the Daimler V8 engines, the HD6 carburettors were mounted at an angle on top of the engine and fed directly into independent inlet manifolds to the cylinder heads. For the 2.5 litre V8 installation a single metal pancake type air cleaner painted silver was mounted on top of the engine, with aluminium curved intakes to each carburettor. For the later V8-250 models, this was changed to twin metal pancake air filters, also silver painted, mounted at an angle on the side of each carburettor. These had a manual choke system similar to that used on equivalent Mk 2 models.

The HD6 installation for the 3.4 litre and 3.8 litre Mk 2s took two forms. The very early cars featured exactly the same arrangement as the 3.4 litre Mk 1, and that included the oil bath air cleaner arrangement.

Within a few months of production (April 1960) a simpler and cleaner system was adopted, and this remained with the cars throughout the rest of their production life. This consisted of a giant pancake-shaped metal air filter box mounted on top of the engine, painted silver and with two flattened trumpet air intakes, each exiting to the side (wing) area. Bolted to a bracket on the cylinder head, the air cleaner was connected to a similar, but differently profiled (oval section) polished alloy intake into the carburettors via a rubber gasket.

The carburettors were fitted with C1 needles and an auxiliary starting carburettor of the same type as the models above.

The 340 engine used exactly the same set-up as the other HD6 equipped Mk 2s except for yet another different air cleaner arrangement. This system used a slightly longer flattened oval box like the 240 but with a single large diameter downward facing intake leading down between the exhaust manifold and the right-hand inner wing.

The S-type used exactly the same engines, carburettors and fuelling as the 3.4 litre and 3.8 litre Mk 2s, the only visible difference being the air cleaner arrangement. Using what was probably the original version of the 340 design, a large black diameter flexible hose directed down between the exhaust manifold and inner wing became the air intake.

The 420 and Daimler Sovereign were the only engines to be

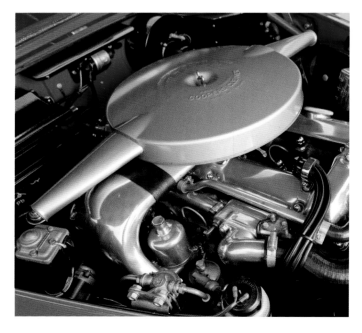

The HD6 installation in the Mk 2 varied from that of the 3.4 litre Mk 1 by changes to the manifold. The same system with different air cleaner arrangement was used on the S-type models as well.

The HD6 carbs on the Daimler engines were mounted at an angle with independent inlet manifolds. This is an earlier installation for the 2.5 litre V8 model.

The later V8-250 engine bay with twin pancake air filters instead of the single unit on the earlier Daimlers.

fitted with the larger (2in diameter) SU HD8 carburettors, of the same type normally seen on the triple-carburettor Mark X and E-type engines. Another new inlet manifold was required for this application with both water passages and balance pipe cast in.

The HD8 carburettors used UM needles and because of their size, a similarly styled but subtly enlarged polished aluminium heart-shaped intake was needed, similar to that used on the other 3.4 litre and 3.8 litre engines. The air cleaner with the paper element took the same form as the 340 and S-types but with a longer metal downward facing air intake that also led to a black flexible hose.

The 240 engine was the only one to use the HS6 SU carburettors but using the same needles as the HD6 carbs. This system also retained a manual choke system.

Twin SU 2in HD8 carburettors were only used on the 4.2 litre engines fitted to the 420 and Sovereign models, requiring another new polished intake.

The twin HD6 carburettors arrangement and inlet manifolding seen from underneath showing the original finishes. Photo courtesy Bob Bate.

Fuel pump

Different types of fuel pump were used in these cars. The SU AUA 57 with a square base was the first (and the same as fitted to the contemporary XK150 sports cars). The SU type AUF 301 was the one used in S-types and later Mk 2s.

Mk 1 and Mk 2 cars had the pumps fitted on two rubber insulators in the left-hand inner rear wing area, behind a millboard panel with an appropriate bulge to cover the extremities of the pumps. The 420 and Daimler Sovereign used a negative-earth version of the AUF 301 pump. The replacement for all these models is the dual polarity pump, type AZX 1308.

The giant 2in carburettor as fitted to the 4.2 litre engine models featured in this publication. Photo by the author.

Fuel filter

From September 1957 engine no. BC.3161 (2.4 litre engines and all subsequent engines from September 1957) a glass bowl type petrol filter was fitted to the inner wing on the inlet side of the engine, with metal fuel lines to the carburettors. All of the SU equipped cars had a small gauze 'acorn' filter inside the top of the float chamber.

Fuel Tanks

All Mk 1s, Mk 2s, 240s 340s and Daimler V8s that utilised the common basic monocoque body structure carried the same 12 gallon fuel tank mounted below the boot floor. This followed the shaping of the spare wheel well. Made of steel and painted black, the tanks were mounted to the bodywork by three rubber insulating mountings. The fuel tank drain plug was opened by the spark plug spanner. Via an access panel in the top of the tank, a simple metal float supplied fuel levels electrically to the fuel gauge in the car. A low-fuel orange warning light was fitted to the speedometer on the dashboard. The metal fuel filler pipe to the tank was accessed via a round, chrome-plated filler cap in the rear wing, with a rubber gasket. From July 1960, a non-vented filler cap was fitted and a fuel breather pipe of black rubber was added to the tank.

S-types and 420s had two saddle-mounted 7-gallon fuel tanks, one per side in the rear wings. Again made of steel and painted black, each had its own fuel filler (alloy with shaped finger grips like the earlier cars) accessed through a lift-up cover in the rear wing. Each tank had its own individual float sensor, and fuel supply to and from each tank was totally independent. Each tank also had its own fuel pump, selected by a switch mounted on the dashboard. No low fuel warning light was fitted.

The single SU fuel pump arrangement for the later Mk 1s and all Mk 2 models. Photo by the author.

COOLING SYSTEM

The cooling system on these engines needed to be efficient due to the limited internal dimensions of the engine bay and the large capacity and physical size of the XK 6-cylinder engines. The situation was not quite so bad with the Daimler V8 units as they took up much less space in the engine bay.

In general use when the cars were new, there were hardly ever any problems, except in very hot climates. Issues arose through not using a corrosion inhibitor in the coolant (such as anti-freeze all the year round), which would lead to major corrosion of the waterways in the cylinder head, or through the silting up of the radiator and/or waterways in the engine cylinder block.

The original 2.4 litre had a narrow cast radiator grille but this allowed insufficient air to circulate for the larger 3.4 litre engine. So a wider grille with narrower slats was fitted, which improved the air intake considerably, and this was subsequently fitted to later 2.4 litre engine models as well. These grilles proved quite satisfactory for their purpose in getting air flow, although they were modified over the years both in style and shape for the Mk 2s and S-types, and there was a complete change of style for the 420.

All the cooling systems were based on a normal pressurised system with a thermostat and belt-driven fan to maintain temperature and air flow.

Radiators

All radiators had steel sides and mounting points, brass top and bottom tanks, and a copper and brass core, all painted black. The original 2.4 litre design had a capacity of 20 pints whereas the radiators in the 3.4 litre and subsequent Mk 2s, S-types, and V8s had a capacity of 22 pints. From late 1964 a larger radiator header tank was fitted.

Entry points for filling were in different positions. Very early 2.4 litre cars had an integrated filler and inlet on the top of the radiator, but from May 1957, followed the 3.4 litre style with separate filler and inlets. All subsequent models except the V8s (where the filler is on the right hand side) used the same principle with the filler on an extension to the left hand

side of the radiator top and with the inlet on an extension to the right hand side. Hoses differed according to each engine application, and except for the V8s, were always on the right hand side of the header tank. On Mk 1s there was a straight exit pipe, which originally had a convoluted hose into the inlet manifold; this was later changed to a curved hose. On the V8s, it was a straight exit from the left hand side of the

The early cooling system fitted to the 2.4 litre model showing the short hose connection between the radiator and water jacket and the siting of the filler to the left-hand side.

The revised radiator and hose arrangement for the Daimler V8 engined models, carried throughout the production of the cars.

The 3.4 litre (Mk 1) radiator installation (also applying to the Mk 2) with the longer water jacket connecting hose and the re-positioning of the filler cap.

A close up of the radiator/hose arrangement on the larger engine models from 1959 on. Photo by the author.

Although the radiator structure for the 240/340 models was basically the same as for the Mk 2, the exit for the top hose arrangement to the water jacket was different.

header tank. In June 1961 the radiator filler cap and neck of Mk 2 radiators were made shallower to aid cooling.

The 240 and 340 models used a full-flow system with an induction manifold that was water heated (instead of being an external part of the layout). The radiator was the same as on the other models, with the inlet on the right hand side and the coolant exit pipe taking the form of an L shape on the left hand side with a special C-shaped hose leading to the inlet manifold water jacket.

From December 1964 a larger capacity radiator block was fitted, which necessitated the use of a revised style of fan cowl.

Both cosmetically and to improve efficiency, the 420 and Sovereign models had a much larger radiator grille, which was similar to but not the same as that fitted to the Mark X of the period. A more efficient crossflow, tube and fin radiator was also employed, with a larger 25½ pint capacity; it was still black painted. This was a conventional radiator but with a silver finished separate header tank bolted on top. The filler for this was positioned directly on top of the header tank with the exit pipe from the left side and a further exit hose on the right-hand side for the top hose. A good point about this system was that it allowed easier fitting of an auxiliary radiator to suit air conditioning in some overseas markets. Air conditioning had only been available before on the Mark X and 420G models, although some systems were fitted by outside companies after delivery of the vehicles.

Radiator caps were all made by AC, zinc coated with a centrally mounted rivet forming part of the spring mechanism. Pressures varied according to engine and specification as well as later changes (see the Production Changes section for full details). Each cap was stamped with the appropriate pressure

The S-type cooling system arrangement was as that of the Mk 2.

and as always, it was important to fit the correct cap for the correct application to avoid over-heating.

Overflow pipes from the filler pipe were always in black rubber, clipped to the side of the radiator frame and leading down to the very base to deposit excess coolant onto the ground.

The completely different and unique cooling arrangement for the 420 and Sovereign models.

The heater controls for the 2.4 and 3.4 litre (Mk 1) models were very primitive, with a simple slider to control the temperature and a black pull button (centre bottom of the dashboard) to operate the booster fan motor.

Twin slider controls operated the temperature control and direction of air. The same system was used on all Mk 2 and Daimler V8 models, supplemented by a two-position toggle switch on the centre dash area for the booster fan motor.

Hoses, Thermostats, Senders and Gauges

All hoses were moulded to their required shape and size, some originally bellows-type but later changed. All hoses were secured to their relevant inlet or outlet pipes by silver coloured jubilee clips, most with screws to secure them in position.

Temperature was controlled by a thermostat fitted in a housing at the forward end of the inlet manifold. Three different types of thermostat were fitted to these models according to specification. A bellows type was used on all the cars featured here except for the 4.2 litre engines fitted in the 420 and Sovereign models. Bellows thermostats were fitted where the thermostat housing comes out of the water rail horizontally. Some early 4.2 litre engines with the long stud cylinder block may have been fitted with a hybrid Thompson type thermostat; in these cases, the housing comes out longitudinally without any extension piece. These Thompson thermostats are no longer available but some companies have introduced a suitable replacement. All other 4.2 litre engines use a common Waxstat thermostat, and in these cases the housing has an extension piece.

As early as 1958 the output pipe in the thermostat housing was enlarged to accommodate a better thermostat.

All cars were fitted with water temperature gauges on the dashboard. On the Mk 1 they were controlled by a capillary pipe with a bulb at the front that screwed directly into the inlet manifold near to the thermostat housing. With the Mk 2 and subsequent models, all had electrical sensors in a similar position.

The Mk 1's gauges were manufactured by Smiths Industries as an integral unit with the oil pressure gauge, calibrated to 100 degrees. Mk 2s up to 1967 and all other models also had a Smiths gauge but now designed as a standalone temperature gauge and calibrated up to 110 degrees. From 1967 the gauge legends were changed so that a simple white band indicated Cool and Normal, and a red section of band indicated Hot.

On the subject of senders all the cars had a petrol gauge sender unit fitted in the top of the fuel tank with two connections, one for the low fuel, and the other to operate the actual fuel gauge.

Water Pumps

The Mk 1 and Mk 2 models, and the 240 and 340, all used a water pump with a 2.75in impellor. The short-stroke 2.4 and 240 models had the heater return pipe at the outside of the pump to allow clearance for the distributor. The earlier models had an alloy casting bolted on to the side of the pump, as on the contemporary XK140 sports car, which was used as a heater return connection. From 1963 the larger engines were fitted with a modified water pump that was more efficient. The later long-stud blocks fitted to the 420 and Sovereign models had a 3in impellor.

Fans and Fan Belts

The fans were made of metal, and had six alloy blades on the early 2.4 engines. From November 1958, a 12-blade metal fan was standardised on all engines. The fan blades were black, all bolts were black, and semi-circular balance weights were attached to those bolts as necessary.

In the 420 and Sovereign engines, the fan had a Holset

On the S-type and 420 models, the heater temperature and air direction were controlled by circular and slider controls built into the parcel shelf area, with the rearward air selection being made by the black switch on top of the transmission tunnel.

All the cars featured here used variations on the same heating and ventilating system with this black metal box containing the matrix, booster fan, etc. On all Mk 1 and Mk 2 models, the box was simply painted black.

viscous coupling which provided a positive drive up to about 2500rpm and above that speed would slip progressively, so minimising power absorption and almost reducing noise. The viscous fan had eight blades and was also finished in black.

The fans were driven by a belt of 10mm size from the bottom pulley on the front of the crankshaft, and this belt also drove the dynamo (or alternator in the case of the 4.2 litre engines) and water pump. Fans are bolted to the water pump flange. The belt size was increased to ½in, and the pulleys were revised to suit, on 3.4 litre engines from January 1959. A notched type was introduced by March 1960 for 3.4 and 3.8 litre engines. From October 1961 a spring loaded jockey pulley was fitted to adjust the belt automatically. A twin grooved fan belt was also fitted from 1962, which necessitated changes to the dynamo, crankshaft and water pump pulleys.

All the fans were accompanied by a fibre-board pre-formed fan cowling attached to the radiator. A very practical addition to diffuse the air generated by the fan into the radiator core, these cowlings were finished in black except on some later models, where they were grey. The style was changed according to the type of radiator fitted.

On S-types, 420s and Daimler models, the heater box was covered in a black fitted Hardura covering.

Heating and ventilation systems

All the models in this book had the same heating and ventilation system, although there was some slight variance in operation for the S-type and 420 models. Made by Smiths Industries, it was quite a basic system with an output of about 3kW. Even by the standards of the day it was a very inefficient system and never that good in real terms, especially compared to the systems available from Ford and others.

This was a fresh-air system that drew air in through the scuttle ventilator at the back of the bonnet tonneau panel. The ventilator was operated manually on all models except for the S-type, 420 and Sovereign, by means of a push/pull lever under the centre of the dashboard. Initially the ventilator was open, but from May 1956 a shroud was fitted to prevent the ingress of water into the rear of the instrument panel. The air was ducted to the fan mounted on the heater box and then onward, via the matrix, to the interior of the car through black convoluted piping that led to the windscreen and below the dash. There was no separate system for the rear compartment, so further pipes ducted the air via the transmission tunnel to the rear, where it exited through a chromed steel grille.

The system consisted of a black painted box mounted in the rear of the engine bay on the left-hand side of the bulkhead.

This was covered in black Hardura on V8s, S-types, 420s and Sovereigns, but left plain black on other cars. It contained the fan blower unit to aid the air being pushed around, and the heater matrix which carried the warm water from the coolant system. The fan unit received its electrical current via a bullet connector from the main wiring loom.

The main heating and ventilating controls were simple sliders that operated Bowden cables. There was one slider on the dashboard on the Mk 1s; Mk 2s and V8s had two sliders on the centre console; and there were chromed knurled knobs on the S-types and 420s. The principle was very simple, with one control handling the direction of the air and the other the degree of heat, its Bowden cable regulating a water inlet valve on the exterior of the heater box that was only introduced in July 1960. Water reached the matrix through black metal piping attached to the bulkhead under the bonnet, and this in turn was fed by black rubber hosing from the inlet manifold water jacket. The connections were secured by jubilee clips.

Heating was further controlled by the electric fan which had two speeds operated by a dashboard mounting switch. Jaguar dealers also used to recommend owners to leave one rear quarterlight open to increase the air flow through the car, a piece of advice that was never given in the handbooks.

EXHAUST SYSTEM

Manifolds

All the exhaust manifolds were made of cast iron and, except in the case of those fitted to the Daimler V8 engines, were finished in black vitreous gloss enamel. Those for the Jaguar XK engines were made in two sections, one per bank of three cylinders, bolted to the cylinder head by 16 nuts and to the appropriate exhaust downpipes with 8 studs.

Although the general style was the same throughout, the actual design and shaping changed to suit the engine configuration. The Mk 1 type was not used on any other saloon models, although it was the same as fitted to the XK140 and XK150 sports models. It had its exits pointing straight down, mated with copper/asbestos gaskets.

The 2.4 litre, 3.4 litre and 3.8 litre Mk 2 manifolds all originally exited downwards, but were different to the Mk 1 in that a shallow chamfer was machined into the manifold to take a 'fire ring', this time using steel and asbestos materials. In and around 1960, production was changed because it was found that the larger engined cars needed swept back manifolds to allow clearance for a power steering pump to be fitted to the

The single pipe exhaust system for the 2.4 litre model exited on the right-hand rear of the car, originally without any chrome finisher. The system depicted here is a modern stainless steel type.

The 3.4 litre engine Mk 1s featured a twin pipe exhaust system also exiting on the right hand side rear of the car. (Author.)

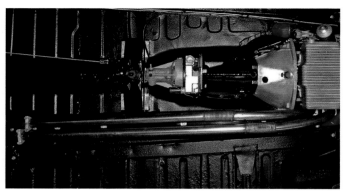

Although this is a later stainless steel system, this view of the underside of a 3.4 litre car shows the correct 'lie' and fitment of the twin pipe exhaust. (Author.)

back of the dynamo. Again a shallow recess, really more of a chamfer, was used. Then from around late in 1961 a deep recess was used to avoid premature failure of the fire ring. The 2.4 litre exhaust manifolds were now the same as those fitted to an E-type. These deeply recessed manifolds were used to the end of production of these models.

The 4.2 litre 420 and Sovereign engines used the same type of exhaust manifolds as the later Mk 2 models.

In the case of the Daimler V8 engines, there was a single separate exhaust manifold for each bank of four cylinders. Each manifold was finished in plain silver and exited slightly downwards.

Exhaust systems

A number of different system designs were used on these cars, all manufactured from mild steel with conventional bracketry and connections. Flange gaskets were used on the downpipes from the exhaust manifolds.

In the case of the 2.4 litre Mk 1 there was a single pipe throughout the system, with one larger silencer. The tailpipe exited underneath the right-hand rear of the car and was not fitted with any chromed finisher. The tailpipe of the 3.4 litre Mk 1 also emerged at the right-hand rear, although in this case there was a twin pipe system throughout with two silencers. From September 1957 production, the 3.4 litre silencers were

In contrast to the early 2.4s, the 2.4 litre Mk 2's single pipe exhaust exited on the opposite side of the car and now boasted a chrome finisher.

All Mk 2 exhaust systems now exited on the left-hand side of the car and had chrome finishers. In the case of 3.4 and 3.8 litre engine models, a twin pipe system was used.

changed to include a greater number of baffles to reduce noise and resonance levels. From November of that year the exhaust downpipes and exhaust pipes were altered for ease of fitment; the downpipes were shortened by 2in while the main pipes were lengthened by the same amount.

For the 3.4 litre and 3.8 litre Mk 2, 240 and 340 models a twin pipe system was adopted throughout, again with twin silencers and again emerging at the right-hand rear of the car. Chromed tailpipe finishers were fitted with shaped ends to match the curvature of the bumper and bodywork in the area. The first 200 cars had their tailpipes chrome plated and welded in place but thereafter a detachable type of chromed trim was fitted. This was modified again in early 1966 with self-tapping retaining screws.

The exhaust system for the Daimler V8s was totally unique, with individual twin pipes running the full length of the underbody independently, one pipe either side of the floorpan. The system emerged at the rear of the car with one tailpipe each side of the car and with chromed finishers.

S-types and 420s used a common system, which was not the same as that fitted to the Mk 2s. Its tailpipes emerged separately at the rear of the car, but relatively close together near the centre under the valance, just inboard of the over-rider positions. Both had upturned chromed finishers.

All Daimler V8 engined cars also featured a twin pipe exhaust system, but in view of the V configuration each pipe was carried independently along the underside of the car to exit on each side at the rear under the bumper.

With the introduction of the Jaguar 240 and 340 models a twin pipe exhaust system was standardised, exiting as shown here.

For the S-type and 420 models, a twin pipe system was also adopted. It combined what had been seen on the Daimler V8s with what was on the larger engined Mk 2.

STEERING, SUSPENSION AND BRAKES

Steering

All these cars were always available with either right-hand or left-hand drive from the factory, and the steering system was mounted on the front sub-frame. All those with manual steering had a Burman recirculating ball system, and so did those with power assisted steering up to early-to-mid 1967. After that, an Adwest power assisted system was used.

The steering box was insulated from the steering wheel and column by a rubber doughnut joint, and all components were finished in black. The top joint was a safety type, known as a pot joint; this utilised nylon rollers in a black steel housing. Later cars with the Adwest steering box had another type of doughnut top joint that would still work if the rubber failed. This later type of column was shorter to allow for the larger steering box. The Adwest models used a different front subframe with a cut-out to take the larger steering box, which was also finished in black paint.

In January 1959 larger diameter lower ball joints were fitted with an increased angle of movement. Re-designed front suspension uprights were also fitted at the same time. From April that year the steering box was amended with lower gearing and both that and the idler drop arms were shortened.

Power assisted steering did not become available until the start of Mk 2 production, when it was introduced as an extra-cost option. However, it was never offered on the 2.4 litre models because there was not enough room for the dynamo-driven power assisted steering pump. This was another Burman product, and it incorporated a Hobourn-Eaton eccentric rotor pump driven off the rear of the dynamo shaft, providing a continuous flow of oil through the hydraulically assisted worm and recirculating ball box. Pressure was only created when the steering was moved, proportional to the effort at the wheel. Cars equipped from new with power assisted steering carried a P prefix to their chassis number.

All the components of the power steering system are painted black, including the metal reservoir with pressure cap fitted under the bonnet on the exhaust side of the engine area. The very first 3.4 litre and 3.8 litre cars were produced with downward facing exhaust manifolds, similar to those fitted to the earlier Mk 1, but as mentioned in the Exhaust section, these were soon changed to the swept back type to provide the clearance required for the PAS dynamo.

The Burman recirculating steering box fitted to a right-hand drive Mk 2 crossmember. The box retains is natural metal colour.

Early Mk 2 front suspension and crossmember installation.

All 2.4 and 3.4 litre (Mk 1) models featured a Bluemels four-spoke steering wheel like this one, finished in blue-black and with adjustable fore-and-aft movement. The centre push activated the horn.

From March 1967, the power assisted steering option for all models changed significantly. A new system of Marles-Bendix design was introduced; developed by Adwest, it was known as Variomatic and was inherited from the later 4.2 litre Mark X saloon. The big advantage of this system was that it applied a varying steering ratio ranging from the equivalent of 4.25 turns lock to lock in the straight ahead position, to 2.1 turns by the time the wheels had reached half lock, resulting in a net figure of about 3 turns lock to lock. On the Mk 2s it was only available through their last months of production, but it remained in use on the 340s, S-types, Daimler V8 250s, 420 and Sovereign models throughout the rest of their production.

Steering wheel and column shroud

Inside the Mk 1 models, a simple black shroud formed a cosmetic cover for the steering column. This led on to a black nylon coated lock nut with finger grips, which allowed the steering wheel to be adjusted fore and aft to suit the driver. The Mk 1s had a Bluemels 17in four-spoke steering wheel which shared its design with other Jaguar saloon models of the time but was smaller. This had a blue-black finish with a centre horn push containing a jaguar's head logo surrounded by two rings, all finished in gold.

For all the other models featured here, the black plastic shroud around the column was of a totally different design. It consisted of upper and lower moulded halves, secured by cadmium finished screws passing through from the bottom to the top section. This shroud also enclosed the stalk mechanisms for the indicators and for the overdrive or

The power steering reservoir was always finished in black, and its positioning is seen here in an S-type.

The first generation steering wheel fitted to all Mk 2 models up to 1964 was also adapted for the earlier 2.5 litre V8 Daimlers with a 'D' motif in the centre. The half horn ring and centre black section activated the horn. (Author.)

Detail fit and finish of the front brake and suspension features relating to the Mk 2. It was the same on most other models featured in this publication. (Photo by courtesy of Bob Bate)

automatic transmission when these were fitted. The upper section of the shroud contained an illuminated Perspex window used for various legends dependent on model (see the Interior Trim section for more details). In November 1962, the upper steering column was modified on export cars to accept the option of a Waso steering lock.

All the later models from the introduction of the Mk 2 used a totally different style of steering wheel with only two spokes and a black plastic finish. There were two types, and in theory the changeover between early and late types occurred in October 1963. However, an unknown quantity of later cars were built with the earlier style of two-spoke wheel, to use up stocks.

The pre-October 1963 steering wheel incorporated a flattened curved section separately attached horizontally across the centre and covering the spokes. Inset in the centre was a small circular plastic badge with a gold jaguar's head against a red background. The post-October 1963 steering wheel was the type already being fitted to the Mark X saloons, and it had a more curvaceous centre section with a larger inset badge. The jaguar's head was also larger, now in gold against a black background with a gold ringed line surround, and the badge doubled as a horn push. (Another production anomaly was that some early examples of this later steering wheel were fitted without the centre horn push operational.) Daimler models had the same steering wheels as contemporary Jaguars, although the inset jaguar badge in the centre was replaced by one with a stylised Daimler 'D'.

Both types of steering wheel incorporated a chromed metal half-horn ring to the lower section; this activated the horns

The later type of steering wheel adopted from the Mark X saloon for Mk 2 and Daimler models, including the S-type and 420. The centre black section of the wheel no longer operates the horn, which is activated by either the horn ring itself or the centre push button containing the Jaguar growler or Daimler 'D'.

The 2.4 litre front suspension and crossmember installation in original finish. (Jaguar Heritage)

either by pushing or pulling on it. Over-exuberant use of this ring could cause it to bend, so that it sat 'inside' the angle of the steering wheel!

Front Suspension

The front suspension remained basically the same throughout the whole production of these models, although detail changes applied according to model and years. All its components were finished in black, except as noted below.

The suspension components were mounted on a front subframe made of steel, which was mounted to the body via a sandwich mounting at the front and V-shaped rubber bonded bushes at the rear. This subframe was quickly detachable and virtually eliminated the problem of noise and vibration being transmitted throughout the car. It consisted of a crossbeam with two arms mounted at right angles to and inboard of the suspension pillars. These arms served to anchor the whole unit to the car's body.

The front suspension was made up of semi-trailing one-piece wishbones, with 14in coil springs, fitted over Girling telescopic shock absorbers with a grey finish. These shock absorbers, both front and rear, were modified to a later design in November 1958 and again in 1963, when a stiffer type was specified. Very early on in production of the 2.4 litre Mk 1, the front springs were lengthened by ⅜in, and then different springs that were 14% stiffer were specified for the 3.4 litre Mk 1. Very early on in production of the 2.4 litre Mk 1, the front springs were lengthened by ⅜in, and then different springs that were 14% stiffer were specified for the rest of production. With the introduction of the 3.4 litre Mk 1, a longer 14 9/16in spring was adopted.

From February 1958, bump stops were added to the front suspension.

The front wishbones on the Mk 2s were initially pressed, but after only a few cars had been produced, they were changed for forged items and angled downwards to move the centre of gravity nearer to the car's roll centre. In April 1960 the spring length was increased by ⅛in and stiffer Girling shock absorbers were fitted.

Rear Suspension

For the rear suspension of Mk 1, Mk 2 and Daimler V8 models, the whole axle was cantilevered from its mountings located in the main structure of the monocoque. Conventional 5-leaf springs (painted black) were used but positioned upside down with trailing arms attached via rubber bushes to fixed extensions on the axle casing, again all painted in a black finish. The springs were anchored to the car inside the ends of the chassis rails. By July 1956 the original fabricated rear mounting plate for the springs was changed for a one-piece pressing.

By September 1956 because of complaints from customers about a cracking noise, synthetic rubber ends were fitted to

the rear spring leaves. Then in May 1958 the rear spring design was altered to provide a change in free camber.

The rear axle was further located by two torque arms running from the rear seat pan to brackets above the axle. These were supplemented by a single Panhard rod which was also finished in black.

There had been concerns about handling on the narrow rear tracked Mk 1s, and so for the Mk 2s the axle casings were extended outwards by 1.625in on each side, which provided a 3.25in width increase in the rear track. Although this was still slightly narrower than the front track, the car now handled better and looked aesthetically more pleasing than the Mk 1s.

The S-type, 420 and Sovereign models featured a version of the Jaguar designed independent rear suspension system, first developed for the E-type and Mark X models introduced in 1961. In these smaller bodies, it was fitted without an anti-

The unusual rear spring arrangement on the cars without independent rear suspension. The Panhard rod (shown incorrectly in red – it should be black) was another unique feature of the suspension set up on these models. (Photo by courtesy of Bob Bate)

The independent rear suspension layout as fitted to the S-type and 420 models. (Photo by courtesy of Bob Bate)

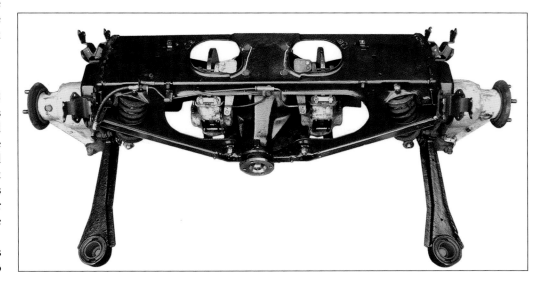

roll bar, and the drive shaft length was somewhere between that of the E-type and the Mark X. This provided a whole new approach compared to the Mk 1 and 2, was much more sophisticated, and provided a better ride quality and handling capability.

The essence of the system was a unique steel cage containing all the suspension, brake and drive link components, which was attached to the body of the car via four V-block rubber mountings. Everything was finished in black. Suspension was provided by a pair of coil spring and damper units on each side of the differential casing, making four in total. These spring and damper units attached to the cage at the top, and to lower links at the bottom. The cage was located to the body by a radius arm on each side, each one running forward from the lower link to a point on the vehicle body and pivoted at each end via rubber bushings and mountings. These arms had a large rubber mounting at the front with voids front and rear to allow a few degrees of movement to facilitate smoother gear changing!

The rear wheels were located transversely by top links, wheel carriers and lower links. The top link was the driving half shaft with a universal joint at each end. The lower link pivoted adjacent to the differential casing at its inboard end and where it met the wheel carrier at the wheel hub casting at its outboard end. The pivot bearings at each end of the lower link were widely spaced so as to provide maximum longitudinal rigidity. The hub carrier, or upright, was left as a bare aluminium casting.

Brakes

All the brakes fitted to these cars are hydraulically operated and have power assistance. For the Mk 1s, Lockheed developed an entirely new system known as BrakeMaster, with self-adjusting 11⅛in drum brakes on all four wheels. The cast brake drums all had a black finish. A master cylinder in natural silver metal finish was mounted in the engine bay in front of the battery area. Very early in 2.4 litre production, both the master cylinder and the reservoir were altered, with the filler cap moving from the front to the right.

The system incorporated a Lockheed 5½in vacuum servo, which was finished in gold and mounted in the front right-hand lower inner wing area. From 1958, disc-braked cars got a larger servo with a diameter of 6⅞in. This necessitated a change in the pedal box design and clutch pedal itself. The servo (and from January 1959 a reservoir) were protected by a shield and mounted on the right side cross member at the front, all painted black. A ⅜in vacuum hose was taken from a metal pipe screwed into the top of the inlet manifold at the rear. From April 1962 a modified brake servo was used, with a two-stage air valve.

For the S-type models a larger 8in brake servo was fitted, and for the 420 and Sovereign models the servo was altered for the dual braking system.

From 1958, Dunlop 12in four-wheel disc brakes became an extra cost option on the Mk 1 models, initially using what was known as the 'round pad' system. With this early system, the wheel cylinders had to be removed in order to change the pads, which was a somewhat tiresome process. So, by January 1959 a new quick-change system that used square pads was fitted, and this system continued into Mk 2 production and beyond.

Calipers at first were zinc plated, then from 1966 cadmium plated. All Dunlop square-pad calipers had flat ended bleed nipples pressing onto a ball bearing seated in a hemisphere in the cylinder, ensuring a positive seal. In 1964 the bleed nipples were repositioned from the outside to the inside of the caliper and the piping was altered to suit. The same revised calipers were initially used on S-types but later changed to a Dunlop type with a single centre retaining pin. In late 1966 they changed again to the 3-pot Girling caliper and ½in discs as on the 420 models. In October 1964 protective shields were fitted to the inside of the brake discs. The front brake caliper assemblies for S-type models were modified in April 1966 to incorporate a bracket and clip securing the hydraulic pipe from the flexible hose union.

The brake fluid reservoir on the early cars was a metal canister on the top of the master cylinder, similar to the clutch reservoir, both being mounted on the pedal box. Later reservoirs were of a round metal type with a low fluid level indicator, made from Bakelite and with two push-on wiring connectors. This was changed to an opaque type from November 1960 on all models. As an aside, drum-braked cars only use DOT 3 brake fluid.

For the cars equipped with the independent rear suspension, the later Dunlop Mk. III system was adopted, with a self-adjusting handbrake mechanism. The discs were now inboard on these cars. Very early S-type models used ⅜in thick rear discs, but in late 1963 ½in thick discs were fitted. Discs on the 420 and Daimler Sovereign were the same as those on the late S-types.

For the 420 and Sovereign models, there were independent hydraulic circuits front and rear, providing a dual-circuit system throughout the car. Power assistance was provided by a Lockheed 4258-447 servo, with two accompanying plastic reservoirs which were mounted side by side, under the bonnet.

All these cars featured the same type of handbrake mechanism with the chromed operating handle positioned to the door side of the driver's seat. The only change was between Mk 1 and the other models; the Mk 1's chrome handle with push-button release was slightly curved, while all other models had a straight handle. Self-adjusting handbrake mechanisms came in for the Mk 2s in August 1961, and the same system was used on all subsequent leaf spring models and was adapted for the IRS models. In March 1966 the retraction plates were redesigned, to improve the alignment of the pad carriers.

TRANSMISSIONS AND REAR AXLES

Manual gearboxes

Only two types of manual gearbox were available on the cars covered in this publication. One was a Moss-derived 4-speed type with synchromesh on the top three gears only, and the other was a Jaguar designed 4-speed with synchromesh on all four gears. Both were available with or without a Laycock de Normanville overdrive that operated on top gear only.

The Moss gearbox was fitted to most of the manual-transmission cars covered in this book – the Mk 1s, Mk 2s and early S-types up to 1964/65. It was based on a single-helical design manufactured by the Moss Gear Company in Birmingham that was used in many cars of the 1940s, 1950s and 1960s. Jaguar Cars took over the assembly of these gearboxes quite early on and this, together with its known longevity, probably explains why it was used in so many Jaguar models.

The designation GB was used for the 2.4 litre, 3.4 litre and early Mk 2 models without overdrive. With this gearbox the tail case is exceptionally long, making it almost equal in length to gearboxes fitted with an overdrive unit.

The serial number is on the top cover, stamped around a large circular ring, and should also be stamped on the left hand side of the main casing in the top rear corner. A suffix of CR, J or MS will indicate that close ratio gearing is fitted. Early examples of the above gearbox fitted to the 2.4 and 3.4 litre models had a cranked gear lever. On the 3.4 litre models a new V mounting was used under the gearbox.

The designation GBN (the suffix N always denoting a gearbox suitable for overdrive fitment) is for the above gearbox when fitted with the Laycock de Normanville overdrive unit operating on 4th gear only. The speedometer drive is on the bottom, angled down and to the right. The top cover has no spacer and does not extend back.

The main casing of the gearbox was cast iron and painted black. The top separate casing was an aluminium casting left in silver finish, as was the rear of the main casing.

The Moss gearbox used in the Mk 1s, Mk 2s and early S-types up to 1965 offered synchromesh on 2nd, 3rd,

and top gears, with or without an additional Laycock de Normanville overdrive that operated on top gear only. Gear ratios changed according to model (see below) and the only differences in appearance were in the positioning and style of gear lever.

From the onset of overdrive being available on the Mk 1s, some cars leaving the factory were equipped with a close ratio gearbox.

For the early Mk 1s, the gear lever was cranked but from July 1958 this was changed to the conventional remote

The Moss four-speed manual gearbox was a standard fitment for most of the cars featured in this book. For the Mk 1 models, a short lever was used like this one, although the very early 2.4 litre models had a cranked lever.

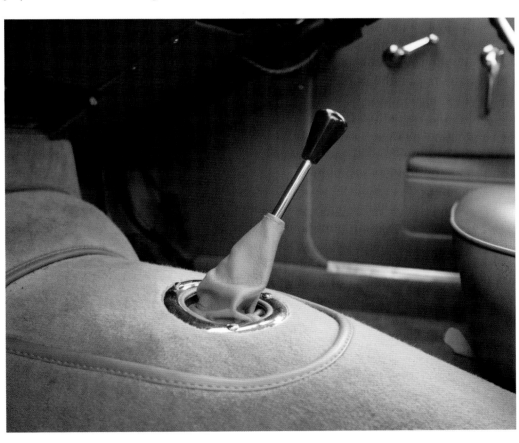

all-synchromesh gearbox for the Mk 2 models, first seen in the E-type, S-type and Mark X a year earlier. Originally an option only for the S-type, it was standardised on this model later. These gearboxes carry the prefix JB (or JBN when fitted with overdrive). The chassis numbers when the change took place on all these cars are shown below in the table. The fitting required a revised diaphragm clutch, a 9½in Borg and Beck type, and longer, self-adjusting slave cylinder, operating rod and adjuster as no return spring was used with the diaphragm clutch. To take this later gearbox the recess in the front of the bell housing was enlarged to 112mm so it would fit over the larger front bearing.

The all-synchromesh gearbox also had a black cast iron casing, with all forward gears having an inertia-lock baulk ring unit that positively prevented engagement before synchromesh was complete. This gearbox was fitted with a round black plastic coated gear knob (without an engraved legend), which was heavier than the pear shaped Moss gear knob to reduce gear lever resonance.

The new all-synchromesh gearbox was fitted from chassis numbers:

2.4 litre	119200 RHD	127822 LHD
3.4 litre	169341 RHD	180188 LHD
3.8 litre	234125 RHD	224150 LHD

The Laycock overdrive unit was an A-type with the Moss gearbox, and then a 'compact A' type was used on the all-synchromesh gearboxes.

Overdrive again operated on 4th gear only which, when specified, required the fitting of a lower ratio rear axle. With the Daimler Sovereign (420) manual model, overdrive was standardised, so there was no non-overdrive option on the manual gearbox cars in this model range. Beginning in March 1969, the overdrive units were fitted with a tapered expansion plug into the rear face of the gearbox.

The overdrive on the Mk 1s was initially operated by a dashboard mounted illuminated plastic switch, but from July 1958 this was changed to a flat black metal toggle switch. On the Mk 2s and other models covered here the operation was from a stalk on the steering column, with an illuminated 'Overdrive' legend in a window across the top of the steering column surround.

Automatic transmissions

In all cases the automatic transmissions were manufactured by the Borg Warner Company at their British assembly facility, so were all marked "Letchworth, Herts". All were of the conventional three-speed torque converter type.

The type DG was fitted to the 3.4 litre model in 1957 and to the 2.4 in 1958. An Intermediate Speed Hold feature was fitted to both these models and was operated from a dashboard mounted black metal switch. As the name implies, this would hold 2nd gear during acceleration, cornering or

Early Mk 2 manual gearboxes, before the all synchromesh type, feature this style of gear lever with a prominent black knob carrying the gear selection legend.

straight type, in the case of all these Mk 1s with a simple black plastic gear knob engraved with the gear positions in white. For Mk 2s and S-types, a different style of gear knob was used, slightly larger in diameter and around the engraved gear selections was a circular white line.

From October 1964 Jaguar introduced their own design of

S-types, 420s, V8-250s and those Mk 2s, 240s and 340s equipped with the Jaguar all-synchromesh manual transmission had a simple round black gear knob.

Of the cars featured here, only the Mk 1s did not have a 'window' and legend on top of the steering column surround relating to the transmission. Cars equipped with overdrive featured the 'overdrive' legend, which up to 1965 illuminated from behind when overdrive was selected. On later models, illumination was merely provided by a small red light as shown here.

The later Mk 1s equipped with Borg Warner automatic transmission had this gear selection control lever fitted to the centre of the dashboard. Made from blue-black Bakelite, it allowed the same installation to be used on RHD and LHD models. The feature was not unique to Jaguar but was used by a few other manufacturers at the time, like Alvis. Jaguar only used it on one other car, the XK150 sports.

on hills. These gearboxes were modified in September 1957 to accommodate a more efficient anti-creep device, and in May 1958 the valve blocks on automatic gearboxes for the 3.4 litre cars were modified to eliminate complaints about jerky changes.

Borg Warner's Model DG was a conventional 3-speed transmission. On the Mk 1 models, it was controlled by a blue-black Bakelite slide handle with a matching surround mounted underneath the centre of the dashboard. It became available from the introduction of the 3.4 litre in 1957, and then was added to the options for the 2.4 litre model as well from 1958. This same transmission was used on all the Mk 2 and S-type automatic models, although with a different selector arrangement (see below).

The DG gearbox was retained unchanged for the Mk 2 range until 1964. However, on these models it was operated by a stalk on the steering column shroud. A pointer in a window on the top of the shroud showed the selector position against a legend of 'R,N,D,L,P', which illuminated when the car's lights were switched on. From April 1966 the operation was modified to incorporate D1 and D2 positions, the latter providing a second gear start. From June 1965 the torque converter was internally modified to improve overall shift quality. These gearboxes are identified by a suffix P in their serial number.

For the Daimler 2.5 litre V8, which was offered only with an automatic transmission, Jaguar chose the Borg Warner Type 35 3-speed unit. This was a lighter unit, which also took up less space and allowed for a lower transmission tunnel in the front compartment of the car. To prevent flexing of the engine and gearbox, the bottom plate of the bellhousing was tied to the sump. These Daimlers were the only models covered in this book on which such a solution was adopted.

In 1965 a later development of the Type 35 gearbox (the Type 35 "plus") was adopted. Initially fitted to the Daimler V8, it was gradually added over a period of time to all the Mk 2 models, eventually becoming the standard automatic fit by the time the 240 and 340 models were introduced. This gearbox eliminated the need for an Intermediate Speed Hold, as the quadrant featured D1 and D2 positions. It was used up to the end of production.

The V8 bell housing was painted black, and for the Mk 2, 240 and 340 models it had a natural aluminium finish, as did the gearbox.

The 420 and Sovereign models had the beefed up Borg Warner Model 8 gearbox made in the United States; its casing was painted black. This stronger gearbox could accept the increased torque of the 4.2 litre engine, and had the D1 and D2 selector positions seen earlier on the Type 35 transmissions. One line of thought was that the D2 position made it easier to set off in snow or icy conditions without wheel spin. The Model 8 was quirky in that the kickdown had a push, not a pull cable to operate it.

Clutches

Borg & Beck supplied all the clutches for these models. The original 2.4 litre car used a 9in single plate hydraulically operated clutch. For the later 3.4 litre engined car the diameter was enlarged to 10in, and this continued on to the 3.4 litre and 3.8 litre models fitted with the Moss gearbox. An 8.5in diaphragm clutch was fitted to the 240 model with the all-synchromesh gearbox. The 3.4 litre, 3.8 litre and 4.2 litre cars all used a 9.5in diaphragm clutch, with the all-synchromesh gearbox. This had a longer slave cylinder with no return spring, an arrangement which Jaguar called "Hydrostatic". This was abandoned in December 1968 on all models, because it required manual adjustment as the clutch wore out.

In March 1969, just for the 340 model, a higher rated diaphragm spring was fitted to the clutch.

Propshafts

The propshafts were made by Hardy Spicer and formed a single piece with connection via a splined tailshaft, rather than the more usual four-bolt flange. With the introduction of the DG automatic gearbox, they used a divided propshaft with a rubber mounted central bearing. These early propshafts all used 2in diameter tube.

Larger propshaft universal joints were fitted from 1961, 82mm instead of 75mm, and a larger 3in diameter propshaft was fitted to all models from 1963 with sealed for life universal joints. The sliding spline still needed lubricating on a service, and 140 grade oil was initially recommended, until grease was found to suit longer service intervals.

The S-type and 420 models in manual gearbox form had a shorter gearbox rear extension housing, which necessitated a longer propshaft with a larger, 3½in diameter.

Rear axles

The axles on these cars were of Salisbury manufacture, and many were the Type 3HA. On the 2.4 litre Mk 1, the 3HA axle ratio was 4.55:1 but from May 1956 it was standardized at 4.27:1. The stronger 4HA axle was fitted to 3.4 litre cars, continuing into Mk 2s with the 3.8 litre engined cars as well. This was also fitted to the 2.4 litre Mk 2s from September 1960 along with the revised propshaft arrangement. The Daimler V8s initially had a 4.55:1 ratio but that changed in June 1964 to 4.27:1.

A Thornton Powr-Lok limited slip differential was standard on the 3.8 litre Mk 2s, and subsequently on the 3.8 litre S-types and the 420s and Sovereigns (although it was dropped from these latter models from March 1967). It was an extra-cost option on the Mk 1 and Mk 2 3.4 litre engined cars, and also surprisingly for export-model 2.4 litre Mk 2s. It was only from January 1965 that the limited slip differential became an option on Daimler V8 models.

Salisbury Transmissions developed the 4HU rear differential for the independent rear suspension S-type, 420 and Sovereign models, although the internal components did not differ from those of the 4HA type, and a Powr-Lok limited slip device was fitted as standard. The differential was solidly mounted into the IRS cage in the centre.

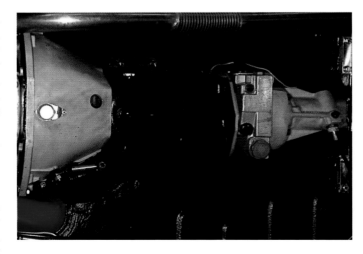

Correct finishes for gearboxes and overdrive units, as depicted underneath this 3.4 litre Mk 1.

WHEELS AND TYRES

All the cars covered in this publication were supplied as standard equipment with conventional five-stud steel wheels, painted to match the body colour. Chromium plated hub caps of different designs were also a standard fit, with the availability of chromed rimbellishers as an extra cost option. Wire wheels were also available as an extra cost option with splined hubs and splined chromed spinners of two types. The wire wheels were available in a choice of body colour, silver painted or chromium plated finishes.

Wheels

With the introduction of the Mk 1 steel wheels were of 4.5J x15 size (ie 4.5in rim width and 15in diameter), and these continued into early Mk 2 production. Then from September 1960 the rims were increased to a 5J size, to allow the fitment of radial tyres. These wider wheels were easily identifiable by an annular depression around the rim. Twelve slots were provided around the centre of the rim to provide brake cooling, and the wheel size is also stamped in the well of the

A standard steel wheel design was used throughout production, although slight differences affected some models (see text). Wheels were always painted in the body colour and carried chromed hub caps. This style with the raised two-eared centre featured on cars up to 1967.

Wire wheels were always a common fit on all models, although they were more popular on some than on others. The number of spokes varied according to year, and the finish could be specified in body colour like this one, stove enamelled silver grey, or chromium plated. Where fitted, the standard two-eared spinner securing nut was like this, although for some markets and the UK later, a non-eared type was fitted.

The later type of wire wheel with more spokes, and chrome plated.

The later type of non-eared retaining nut for the wire wheeled cars. Again badging changed to suit a Jaguar or Daimler model.

spats of the 2.4 litre model, and so Jaguar developed cut-away spats. Wire wheels were expected to be popular on the 3.4 litre, and so these cars had the cut-away spats as standard. Subsequently any 2.4 litre models fitted with wire wheels also used the cut-away spats, which later replaced the full spats as standard on this model as well.

Initially the wire wheels had a total of 60 spokes but for all models were standardised at 72 spokes from January 1959. From March 1967 the wire wheel centre hubs were forged with a more pronounced shaping and with straight spokes. These have become commonly known as 'easy clean' wheels because the shaping makes them easier to keep clean! The early type are now known as the 'curly hub' type for obvious reasons.

On cars with wire wheels, splined hubs were fitted to accept the splined inner face of the wire wheel centre. The wire wheels were then secured to the axle hubs by splined 'spinners' in a chromed finish, which screwed onto the car's hubs forcing the inner face of the wheel against them. There were two different styles of spinner fitted, each with two different insignias: "Jaguar" or "D" for Daimler, according to model, in both cases cast into the face of the spinner and painted black. The cars with the 'curly hubs' up to March 1967 featured the two-eared type of spinner where the protruding sections were used to tighten down the spinner with an appropriate mallet or hammer. However, as early as 1959, cars destined for Germany had to have a non-eared spinner fitted to meet safety regulations; some other markets followed this lead later, and this type of spinner was eventually standardised on all cars to meet new legislation. To remove this spinner, a cast bronze spanner was fitted over it, and the spinner was tightened or loosened by the use of a hammer on the outer lugs of this so-called 'spinner spanner'.

All cars carried a spare wheel as standard equipment under the boot floor in the special wheel well provided. Of the same size, specification and tyre fitment as the other wheels and tyres, it was fitted face down in the well and secured in position by a black painted threaded bolt and clamp passing through the centre of the hub to a similarly threaded bracket welded in the floor.

The first few 2.4 litre cars produced had a clamp of a different shape that did not secure the wheel sufficiently, so this was changed to the one used throughout the rest of production. By fitting the spare wheel face down, it was possible to fit the comprehensive tool roll in this area (see the Tools and Handbooks section).

Trims

All steel wheel equipped cars were fitted with chromed plated hub caps, the interior face of which was red lead painted. Three types of hub cap are known to exist, the two original Jaguar fitments and one produced in South Africa under the agreement for the knocked down kits of cars supplied to

rim. For the 420 and Sovereign models, 5.5J wheels were specified, and these were later adopted for all cars from July 1967 as a standardisation exercise.

It was not until the introduction of the 3.4 litre model that centre-lock wire wheels became available as an extra cost option. These could not be fitted behind the full rear wheelarch

Revised Daimler badging on the later type of hub cap.

Daimler models featured their own scripted 'D' within the hub caps. Daimlers were also fitted with chromed rimbellishers like this one shown here, an extra cost option on Jaguar models.

contain a degree of local manufacture.

The initial style of hubcap was exactly the same in style and shape as those used on all Jaguar models from 1948, featuring a bevelled edge and raised centre section with a two-eared design incorporating a two-bolted centre 'Jaguar' emblem with a black background. The only difference from the other Jaguar models was that none of the cars featured here had a body-coloured inlay and a double bevel edge (even though the very early 2.4 litre brochure artwork showed this). This initial type of hubcap continued to 1967 when, with the introduction of the 240 and 340 and other model changes affecting the S-type, 420 and Daimlers, a new, simpler style was adopted. Of the same proportions, this second type of hubcap had a less pronounced lip but deeper centre section containing a single black background circular emblem, either containing the jaguar head or the scripted 'D'. Both emblems were secured by a single stud and nut.

For the South African cars, and also for export areas at the time like Rhodesia, the 'home grown' product was even simpler than the original Jaguar style, without the eared sections.

Tyres

The original specification tyres for these cars were Dunlop tubeless RS3, size 6.40 x 15 cross ply. From April 1958, RS4s became the standard fit on 3.4 litre cars. Dunlop RS5s of the same size became the later standard fit on Mk 2s and S-types with the options of Dunlop SP41 radials of 185 x 15 size, or SP3 as a performance radial option. Most people however did take the radial option. The SP41 became the standard fit on S-types from June 1964.

With the introduction of speed ratings, SR was recommended for 2.4 litre models, HR or VR for 3.4 litre and 3.8 litre cars.

With the introduction of the revised model ranges in 1967, a new style of hub cap was adopted for all cars. It had more pronounced outer and inner shoulders, and a circular growler badge was used on Jaguars.

ELECTRICAL SYSTEM AND EQUIPMENT

These cars all used a standard 12-volt electrical system with the majority of components supplied by the British Lucas company. All those cars fitted with a dynamo were positive earthed.

Dynamo and Alternator

The majority of the cars featured here generated electricity from a Lucas dynamo driven by a fan belt. The dynamo was bolted to the XK engines on the exhaust side and had a three-point mounting with an adjustable slide to ensure the correct belt tension. All components would have been in black finish. In the case of the V8 engines the dynamo was fitted on top of the engine mounted direct to the cylinder heads.

The original dynamo was a Lucas type C45 PVS-5 but in May 1959 a new 25-amp dynamo was fitted (the C45 PVS-6) which required an amended regulator, an RB310, the original being an RB106. In February 1962 a high output

C42 dynamo was fitted to 3.4 litre and 3.8 litre models, and shortly afterwards to 2.4 litre models as well. From April 1963 an uprated C48 dynamo could be had to special order, and when fitted this was accompanied by a new control box, the RB340 (Lucas 37354/F).

Alternators did not begin to be fitted until the introduction of the 420, and replaced the V8's dynamo in September 1967. The alternator was type 11AC, with a 4TR control box and a 3AW ignition warning lamp control unit. (Some Police Specification 340 models were fitted with a 10AC alternator).

Starter motor

The Lucas type M418G starter motor was fitted to 2.4 litre models, always finished in black. The 3.4 and 3.8 litre cars used an M45G starter. In December 1968 the previous Lucas starter solenoid, with a rubber push button, was replaced by the later type which did not have one.

The general layout of the 2.4 litre (Mk 1) engine bay, showing the lie of the plug leads with their correct chromed 'separator', and the bulkhead mounted starter solenoid and control box.

Wiring detail of the 2.4 and 3.4 litre early cars. Note the protective 'shelf' in metal, painted black, protecting the wiring from ingress of water when the bonnet is raised; the control box has been removed from this position. The large black knob on the battery connection is a non-standard isolation device, but period to the car.

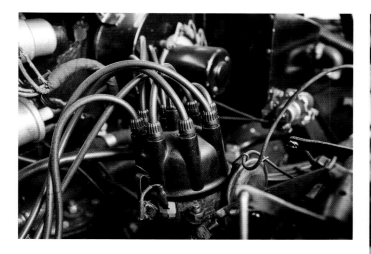

The distributor is sited at the rear on the V8 engines.

Voltage Control Box

Voltage regulation was dealt with by another Lucas product, initially the RB106 on the 2.4 litre model. Mounted on the exhaust side of the engine bay on a black metal bracket and baseplate, the relays were protected by a black metal cover, bolted through to the baseplate.

With the introduction of the 3.4 litre model, this changed to the standard Lucas RB310 control box with a natural aluminium cover. The RB340 version was fitted from early 1963 onwards.

Ignition coil

The ignition coil on the XK engines was always mounted horizontally on a saddle bracket attached to the front of the engine cylinder head, and on the V8 engines it was horizontally against the bulkhead in the centre position. Always in natural aluminium colour for the coil and bracket, the type of coil was the HA12. The nose of the coil was in black Bakelite (later conventional plastic), with a threaded knurled knob holding the high-tension lead from the distributor, although many later cars (from the 340 on) had a simple push-on connection. All Lucas coils have their date of manufacture stamped on their base.

Distributor and Ignition leads

The distributor was again a standard Lucas design. The 2.4 and 3.4 litre cars used a DM8ZA unit. With a 7:1 compression ratio, the 2.4 was equipped with a 40557 and with the 8:1 compression a 40528 was fitted. The 3.4 with a 7:1 compression ratio used a 40578, with 8:1 a 40576, and with 9:1 a 40617. (The very early 7:1 compression engines were fitted with a 40528 unit). Later cars have a 22D6 with a push-on vacuum connection.

The plug leads entered the cap from the top and were of black finish. The spark plug connectors on the other end of

the leads were also black hard plastic, and originally would have carried the Champion brand name on each, embossed with white paint. Rubber caps in black were fitted to all plug leads and HT leads where they entered the distributor from August 1963. Then in June 1965 a black waterproof 'gasket' was added to the distributor cap to help prevent ingress of dirt and damp.

The leads were assembled into a neat conduit covering made of charcoal coloured fibre board that rested in the 'valley' of the cylinder head and was secured by two brackets riveted onto the conduit; each bracket was held in position by two cylinder head nuts. At the forward end of the engine, each lead passed through a circular black plastic 'separator', with a chrome-plated steel clip surround. This surround was secured to one of the forward cam cover nuts, and was changed to

Later bulkhead electrical detail on the 240/340 models.

Wiring looms on the cars were bound in this way and secured around the engine bay by plastic covered clips.

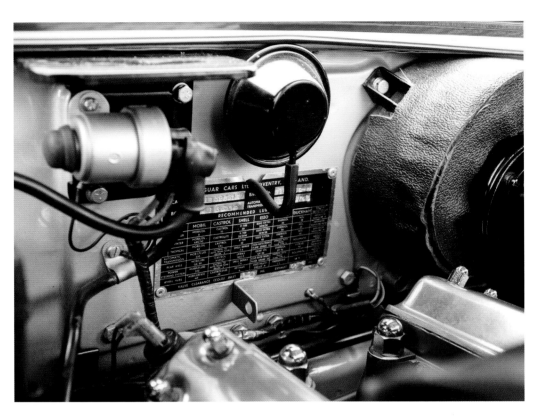

Engine bay bulkhead detail of the S-type and 420 models shows the chassis plate re-positioned from the inner wing area.

Ignition Timing

2.4 litre and 3.4 litre	Champion L7 (or L10S) for 7:1
2.4 litre (Mk 1)	4 degrees BTDC (7:1 compression)
	6 degrees BTDC (8:1 compression)
3.4 litre (Mk 1, Mk 2, S-type & 340)	TDC (7:1 compression)
	2 degrees BTDC (8:1 compression)
	TDC (9:1 compression)
2.4 litre Mk 2	6 degrees BTDC (7:1 compression)
	8 degrees BTDC (8:1 compression)
3.8 litre Mk 2 and S-type	TDC (7:1 compression)
	7 degrees BTDC (8:1 compression)
	5 degrees BTDC (9:1 compression)
240	12 degrees BTDC
420	8 degrees BTDC (all compressions)
2.5 litre (V8)	10 degrees BTDC

black plastic from 1966. After passing through the separator, the leads dropped down to the distributor. In September 1963 for the 3.4 and 3.8 litre engines, the plug leads were lengthened to accommodate a revised run around the cam covers.

The firing order was 1-5-3-6-2-4 for all the XK engines and 1L-4R-2R-2L-3R-3L-4L-1R for the Daimler V8 engines.

Spark Plugs

Original equipment spark plugs recommended by Jaguar were as follows:

2.4 litre and 3.4 litre	Champion L7 (or L10S) for 7:1 compression engines.
	Champion N5 (or NA8) for 8:1 and 9:1 compression engines.
3.8 litre	Champion N5 (all compressions)
3.4 and 3.8 litre S-type	Champion UN12Y (all compressions)
4.2 litre	Champion N11Y (all compressions)
2.5 litre (V8)	Champion N8

Ignition timing

Static ignition timing varied from model to model (see below). Ignition timing was advanced automatically, both by centrifugal weights within the distributor and by vacuum advance.

Horns

All these cars were equipped with two-tone (high note and low note) electric horns supplied by Lucas. On the Mk 1s these were of the HF1748 type of 'flat' design painted in silver, and provided a strident deep tone typical of cars from the era of the 1950s.

After the Mk 2 had been in production for a few months, horns on all Jaguar models were standardised to the black finished Lucas type 618U offering an even more strident conventional sound. These quite bulbous horns were in turn replaced on all models by the flat black plastic 9H type (known as Windtone horns) in April 1966.

Each horn had a black bracket with two holes to bolt it to the body.

Windscreen wiper and washers

These models all used a Lucas DR.3 wiper motor with a natural silver finish, which was mounted on the inlet side of the XK engine bay. The system had a two-speed setting with a self-parking device. All motors carried a date of manufacture. Internally the wiper motor was strengthened and fitted to all later Mk 1 models and beyond.

The system operated via a cable, with two spindles mounted through the scuttle tonneau panel to chromed arms and blades. The motor and arms were 'handed' according to market so that the blades always parked on the driver's side.

On the Mk 1s, the wipers were operated via a black circular plastic switch on the dashboard and on the other models by a two-position black plastic toggle switch on the dashboard centre panel.

All models were fitted as standard with a screen washer system with twin chrome jets fitted onto the scuttle tonneau panel, controlled either by a small chrome push button on the dashboard of the Mk 1s, or by a black toggle switch on the dashboard centre panel of all other models.

The Mk 1 system was vacuum-operated and was supplied

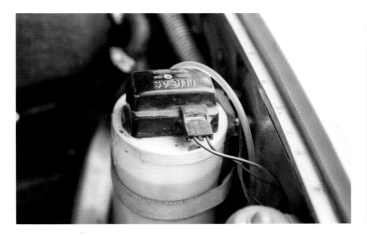

A totally different type of screen wash motor assembly was fitted to the later cars, including S-types and 420s.

Various under-bonnet ancillaries were relocated when the 4.2-litre engine was installed in the 420 models.

by Wipac. It had a large circular glass reservoir bottle mounted on the exhaust side inner front wing under the bonnet, secured by a black metal bracket to the wing. The reservoir had a black metal screw top with a circular stick-on Wipac label (with white lettering on a background that was half red and half black), along with two take-offs, one centrally mounted, the other to the edge of the top to supply fluid to the system. Black rubber hosing carried the fluid along the side of the exhaust side inner wing area and along the bulkhead scuttle to the jets. Vacuum was taken from the inlet manifold to the other side of the washer bottle, and a chrome plated button the dashboard caused the washers to work for several seconds when pressed and released. A single push on the dashboard mounted button would activate the water jets for a set time.

For all other models an electric Trico system was adopted from 1959, and this continued through virtually unchanged until 1965. It consisted of a large square glass bottle with similar black

bracketry in the same wing area at the Mk 1s, but with a substantial black circular plastic screw fit top which contained the operating motor under a black plastic cover. The name and model type were in relief on the top, and there were spade connections from which the electric wires connected to the control box. The plastic top of the bottle also incorporated a rubber flap to enable fluid to be added without unscrewing the whole top, and a plastic upright take-off for the transparent plastic piping to the jets.

From April 1965 all models were fitted with the Lucas 5SJ system, the differences being a change-over from glass reservoir bottle to a high density white plastic type of an oval design. This was secured to the wing area by a fabric type stretched band to a clip on the inner wing area. A circular white plastic cap was fitted to fill the bottle with fluid and the same black motor and casing were employed as before but with a flat push-fit black connector for the electrical wires.

The later type of control box arrangement fitted to Mk 2s and later models.

With the changeover to a negative earth system on all cars, the battery retaining bracket was fitted with a warning notice.

This system operated differently in that it only remained active as long as the toggle switch on the dashboard was held up in the 'on' position.

Wiring

All cars up to the 420 were wired with a positive-earth system, and only the 420 and Daimler V8-250 had a negative-earth system. The wiring loom was made in several sections and where necessary joined by either bullet or spade connections. As is normal practice, colour-coded wiring was used and was wrapped in a braided black patterned covering.

The colour coding for the wiring, used in schematic diagrams, was as follows:

B = black, U = blue, N = brown, R = red, P = purple, G = green, S = slate, W = white, Y = yellow, D = dark, L = light and M = medium. When a cable had two colour code letters, the first denoted the main colour, the second the tracer colour.

Wiring looms were installed externally in the engine bay secured to the exhaust side inner wing area by plastic coated P-clips and then through the bodywork including the inner sill areas.

The wiring incorporated a fuse box, a Lucas SF6 which was mounted in the engine bay on the black base plate alongside the control box and under a black square shaped cover with black knurled knob to secure. Two glass cartridge type fuses were used and two spares fitted. These originally had a 35 amp rating, and in later Mk 1s 50-amp fuses were used. Not all electrical items in the car were fused, and changes took places throughout production (see the section on Production Changes).

In September 1965 the main wiring loom was amended

and a hazard warning light system operated from a switch on the driver's side dashboard panel was fitted to export models as standard equipment. It was available for others as an extra cost option.

Battery

All these models were fitted from new with one standard oblong battery No. 54028491 – BV.11A, supplied by Lucas. It had a hard black rubber casing and tar tops, and was mounted on the bulkhead on the inlet side of the engine bay with the lead push-on terminals facing the front. Lead terminal connections were of the helmet type carrying the + or – connection identification in relief and with screw connections to the terminals.

The batteries were fitted to a black plastic moulded tray which just rested on the metal bulkhead 'shelf'. The tray had a lip and an exit point for water to drain, with a black rubber drainage pipe reaching down the side of the bulkhead. This drain tube was found to be too short to do its job effectively, so was increased in size from April 1965.

The battery was secured in position by a black bracket running across its width at mid-point, curving to follow the line of the battery sides, to bolt connections to the bulkhead. The bracket had a ribbed centre section and carried a rubber insert. On negative-earth models, the bracket also carried a square identification panel in the centre with a label confirming the earthing type. From the introduction of the Mk 2 (and all subsequent models) a black plastic moulded top was also fitted to the battery, of a sloping design with cut-outs for the battery connections and spring metal clips to secure it to the battery top sides.

The battery position on all models was against the bulkhead in the engine bay as shown here. This period battery is typical of those fitted and displays the black metal securing bracket wrapped around the middle which should have a rubber insert to prevent chafing. Quite often missing from the cars is the black plastic protective cover over the battery to prevent ingress of water when the bonnet is opened...

...and here is the correct battery top cover in place. Both this and the securing bracket are now available as re-manufactured items because most originals were discarded by owners years ago.

LIGHTING

All the lighting for these cars was supplied by Lucas. Some items were interchangeable with other models and other marques, but some were unique to these particular models. Some unusual changes had to be made for certain overseas markets, but it is not possible to cover all of these here.

Headlamps

For the Mk 1 models and Mk 2 cars up to early 1960, Lucas 51767 / F700 flat faced 7-inch headlamps were fitted, requiring separate 42/36watt bulbs. Before that however, in July 1958 60-watt headlamp bulbs were standardised on all UK cars. Interestingly cars destined for the US market were shipped without headlamps, and locally-sourced sealed beam units were fitted in the USA. Although obligatory there, they were not yet available in the UK. From 1959, 60/36watt bulbs were standardised for all left-hand-drive cars.

From September 1962 conventional sealed beam headlight units were fitted to all cars; these were Lucas 59310/F700. In May 1963 due to ingress of dust, a rubber dust excluder in black was fitted to right-hand side headlights. By December 1968 standard European lighting had been adopted for left-hand-drive cars, following which headlamp types were then unchanged throughout the rest of production.

The headlamp units were fitted in metal bowls painted black with three spring-loaded adjustment screws over which the clamping rings that held the lamp were fitted. The bowls were attached to the body by cross-headed self-tapping screws and there was a black rubber gasket between the headlamp bowl flange and the car's body. Moulded into this were hollow tubes with closed ends that covered the ends of the adjustment screws, protecting their threads from road dirt and corrosion.

For Mk 1s, Mk 2s and Daimler V8s, each headlamp had a chromed beveled rim fitted over it from the top. A rivet was slipped over the projections of the headlamp bowl and the rim was then secured at the bottom centre by a chromed self-tapping screw.

The fitting was different for the S-types, 420 and Sovereign models because the chromed rims were shallower but with a peak at the top. These rims clipped in the headlamp assembly at the bottom, and were secured at the top centre by a chromed self-tapping screw directly into the peak of the car's

The lighting layout for 2.4 litre and 3.4 litre (Mk 1) models shows the overall side light lenses unique to these cars, the conventional Lucas headlamp units and the Lucas Fogranger pod mounted fog lamps.

The later more common type of headlight units fitted to all models.

Close up of the flat-faced headlight units used on the earlier Mk 2 models.

Side lamps, indicators and reflectors

All this lighting was unique to the Jaguar brand and some to specific models featured here.

Front sidelights and indicators

The Mk 1 was certainly unique as no other Jaguar model or other car featured the vertical oval style of combined front indicator and sidelight that was fitted. Produced for Jaguar by Lucas, (type 52264/L566), these had a plain frosted glass lens with a chromed surround and rubber gasket which was held in place by pressure. The light unit itself was of the usual metal construction holding a 6/24-watt type 380 bayonet-fit bulb which acted as both the side light and flashing indicator light. The assembly was backed by a pre-formed black rubber gasket surround which also encompassed the bulb holder and wiring inlet. The assembly was held in position to the lower area of each front wing by two self-tapping screws.

For the Mk 2s and Daimler V8s there was a totally different arrangement with separate side lights and indicators. The sidelights were the same as used in the later XK120s, Lucas L490 with part number 42474/B. They had a single circular frosted glass lens with a fixed chromium surround with a top clip; a chromed screw passed through this to secure the unit to the front wing 'pod' of the car. The bulb was a 4-watt type 222, in a bulb holder fixed to the light unit securing bracket. These light units are interchangeable with those on the early XK120 sports models, but not those on the XK140s or XK150s.

A separate feature to these side lights was the red tell-tales affixed to the front wings. Each tell-tale was a moulded red plastic rectangular shaped lens that slotted through a hole in the top of the wing, secured in place by a spring metal clip.

bodywork headlamp surround. The difference between the S-type application and that on the 420 and Sovereign was that the latter were fitted with a four-headlamp arrangement, with 5-inch inner headlamp units and 7-inch outer headlamp units. Due to different legal requirements in most US States, only the 5-inch light units were allowed, so to accommodate this the outer headlights for these markets had the same 5-inch units as the inners. Because of the larger aperture in the bodywork, a different, deeper style of chrome trim was required.

The headlights on S-types had a peaked chromed surround, and so did the fog lamps, which were of a different design to those fitted to Mark 2s, 240/340 models, and Daimler V8s. The side light and indicator units were of the same design as fitted to Mark X models from 1961. The wrap-around orange plastic lens made the indicators more visible to other motorists.

The introduction of the 420 and Sovereign models saw a further rationalisation and modernisation process to match other Jaguar models. As well as the adoption of the S-type side light and indicator units, the four-headlight style of the Mark X/420G was used. All headlights now featured peaked chromed surrounds set into the bodywork, although they were different to those on the S-type.

With the introduction of the Mk 2 range the lighting was amended, primarily to satisfy changing legislation. Orange (or white for certain markets) indicator lenses were now fitted to the bottom of the front wings and were common to other Jaguar models of the time. The side lights were mounted on pods extending from the top of the front wings. Moving the fog lamps was necessary so from this time they were of a revised Lucas type rear mounted through the wings onto a chromed backing so that they could be swivelled into appropriate positions.

When the lights were on, they reflected the light so that the driver could see that each side light was actually working. There has been much discussion over the years about the way these reflectors were fitted to the cars when new. As they have the name Lucas embossed in the top and were shaped, they should have the slope facing towards the front of the car, at which time the Lucas name can be read. Some cars, however, certainly left the factory with the reflectors fitted the other way round!

The separate indicator lights on the Mk 2s and Daimler V8s were fitted in the same position as the combined units for the Mk 1s. They took the form of a standard Lucas 3-inch circular orange glass lens (plain lenses were used in some overseas countries) held in place by a chromed surround and rubber gasket. The surround was fixed to the light housing by means of a top mounted chrome self-tapping screw. The light unit comprised a conventional metal assembly containing a 21-watt bulb and an inclusive gasket for the bulb holder and wiring entry point. The unit was secured to the front wing by means of two self-tapping screws.

The S-type, 420 and Sovereign models had another different style, with an integrated side light/indicator assembly that was the same as that used on the larger Mark X and 420G models. There was a small circular clear frosted lens for the side light, and a curved elongated orange plastic indicator lens curved around to the side of the front wing. Both were secured to the light unit by means of chromed self-tapping screws, with chromed surrounds and rubber gaskets. The units had a pre-formed gasket at the rear covering the bulb holder and wiring inlet, and were secured to the front wing by a single self-tapping screw.

Rear Lighting

Three types of rear light units were fitted to the cars covered here, totally different for Mk 1s, Mk 2s and V8s, and S-types, 420s and Sovereigns.

The Mk 1 rear lights used a standard Lucas type 574635 red plastic lens, incorporating the reflector, but the actual plinth was unique because it was shaped to match the slope of the rear wings of the car. The lens was fixed to the holder by two chromed self-tapping screws, one at the top and one at the bottom. Made from Mazak and chromed, the light unit contained just one bulb, a 6/21watt type 380 that acted as both rear/stop light and flashing indicator. The plinth was attached to the car via a shaped black rubber gasket and held in position by two self-tapping screws through the casing.

Legislative changes meant that the Mk 2s and Daimler V8s

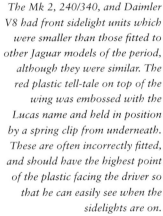

The Mk 2, 240/340, and Daimler V8 had front sidelight units which were smaller than those fitted to other Jaguar models of the period, although they were similar. The red plastic tell-tale on top of the wing was embossed with the Lucas name and held in position by a spring clip from underneath. These are often incorrectly fitted, and should have the highest point of the plastic facing the driver so that he can easily see when the sidelights are on.

The rear light units for the Mk 1 models incorporated stop, tail and indicator lamps plus reflectors in a single red plastic lens. They were typical of the period and were fitted to a significant number of other cars. However, the Mazak chromed plinth was unique to these Jaguar models, because of the styling of the rear wings.

Rear light units for the S-type and 420 models were of the same design as those fitted to the Mark X and its 420G successor. Each element had its own plastic lens as on the Mk 2, but their shapes were different.

Rear lighting adopted for all Mk 2, 240, 340 and Daimler models had separate indicator lamps, again through changing legislation. The new units were larger, with individual lenses and more prominent reflectors on extended chromed Mazak plinths. The lenses were common to other Jaguar models of the period but the plinths were unique to these cars.

had to have separate lights for indicators and rear/stop lights, so Lucas produced a new design, type L627 (LH 53726/A, RH 53727). The rear wing shape again ensured that these were unique to the model, although similar styles were made for the later XK150 and Mark IX models. The lenses were in three parts, all of plastic and interchangeable with the light units fitted to the other models mentioned above. The top lens was orange for the indicator for most markets, but clear for others; the middle lens was separated from above by a chromed rib, and was in red for the rear/stop light. The two formed a single unit held in position by chromed self-tapping screws. The bottom section formed the reflector, circular and an integral part of the light unit itself with a chromed surround.

The shaped plinth was made of Mazak and chromed. It was held to the car's bodywork via a rubber gasket to a bracket and ¼-inch UNF stud, and a captive ¼-inch UNF bolt. The plinth formed part of the bulb holder, again in Mazak, and there were two bulbs. The flasher bulb was a 382, and the stop/tail bulb a 380.

The S-type, 420 and Sovereign models used the same rear light unit as the Mark X/420G and the Daimler DS420 limousine, made of the same materials and to the same format as the Mk 2 light units, but of a totally different shape to match the style of the rear wings.

As with the front lights, some overseas markets required indicator lenses that were clear instead of orange.

The rear number plate light unit in chromed Mazak was used throughout Jaguar production of the Mk 1, Mk 2, and 240/340 models. The centrally mounted reversing light lens was glass and featured the embossed Jaguar name.

With the addition of the Daimler variants to the Mk 2 range, a new ribbed rear number plate/reversing light unit was designed. Although it included the same type of glass reversing light lens as the Jaguars, there was now a scripted Daimler name.

The standard rear number plate surround used on the S-type and 420 models was modified to take a plastic Daimler emblem in black with gold script, bolted through the plinth.

Close up of the chromed surround design of the Lucas foglights fitted to Mk 2s.

Flasher Unit

To operate the indicators, a Lucas type FL5 flasher unit was used. This was a simple cylinder-shaped alloy-finished sealed unit, secured to the dashboard behind the centre panel by self-tapping screws. Most later cars for export markets also had a hazard warning system on the later cars.

Auxiliary Lighting

The only model among those covered by this book which did not have auxiliary lighting as standard equipment was the 2.4 litre Mk 1 Standard model, which never actually went into production even though it was listed. However, for some overseas markets auxiliary lighting was not permitted, so the cars were dispatched without any, and with appropriate changes to the light switch on the dashboard.

The Mk 1s had two Lucas Fogranger light units fitted which were a common fit by other manufacturers and indeed as after-market accessories. Of the type 55174/D-SFT576, complete with their standard 'pods', they were fitted to the horizontal metal panel forming the cross-brace between the two front wings. An option was to fit one Fogranger and one Spotranger light by special request.

For the Mk 2s and Daimler V8s, Lucas Fogranger lights were also used but of a new design (type 5WFT, part number 55262/A). These were mounted into the front wings via special chromed mountings, secured in position by a single black painted nut and bolt through the wing. The curvature of the rear of the light and its mounting allowed a certain degree of adjustment. The chromed surround was initially ribbed, but a plain type was used later. These light unit surrounds were unique to the Jaguar range but similar types were fitted to other cars like the Vanden Plas of the period.

The auxiliary lighting for the Mk 2s was deleted as a standard fit from September 1966, although it remained standard on Daimler models up to the end of production and could be ordered as an option on the Jaguars?. In place of the lights, a circular chromed Mazak mock horn grille was fitted with vertical ribs and a jaguar head emblem in the centre. This type of grille was also fitted to export models that were not equipped with auxiliary lighting.

Note that the grilles fitted to all Mk 1 models were of the same type as those used on other Jaguar models like the Mark VIIM to IX. These had a thick centre vertical rib. The mock grilles fitted to Mk 2s and V8s when auxiliary lighting was not fitted were of a different style and so are not interchangeable.

Moving on to the S-type, these cars were also fitted with Lucas Fogranger lights, but without a chromed surround. Instead they were flush-mounted into the front wings and secured in a similar way. Again for some overseas markets and for all cars from September 1966, the auxiliary lighting was deleted except to special order. The mock horn grilles

The very last Mk 2 models and all subsequent 240 and 340 models were not fitted as standard equipment with fog lamps. Instead, this type of mock horn grille was adopted. The installation was also found on earlier cars for some overseas markets, due to legislation.

For certain overseas markets, the Lucas fog lamps were not fitted. They would not have been fitted to the 2.4 litre Standard model if it had ever been produced, either.

fitted to S-types were different again, this time flush styled.

The Jaguar 420 and Daimler 420 Sovereign were not fitted with auxiliary lighting as standard but did have a form of mock horn grille. This had a rectangular chromed style with inset mesh.

Interior lighting

As mentioned in the Dashboard section earlier, all instrumentation had internal lighting. Additional lighting in the interior varied in type according to model and year.

For the Mk 1 range, two interior light units were fitted in the rear quarters of the roof area above the parcel shelf. Both had standard bulbs and a clip mounted opaque white plastic cover. The light units were let into the headlining, as shown in the picture.

There were no fewer than four interior light units in the Mk 2 interior. Two circular frosted units with chromed surrounds were mounted into the rear quarters of the headlining, and a further two rectangular frosted lights with chromed surrounds were fitted to the top of the B/C post area within the shaped wood trim. All four were operated from the switch on the dashboard. The lights on the B/C posts were another item shared with other Jaguar saloon models of the time.

The Daimler V8s had the two B/C post mounted lights and just one of the same type mounted centrally at the rear of the headlining near the rear screen area. The S-type and 420 models had the same treatment as the Daimler V8s.

240 and 340 models were equipped with these dummy horn grilles instead of fog lamps, although the latter could still be specified as an extra cost item.

DASHBOARD, INSTRUMENTATION AND CONTROLS

There were only two styles of dashboard layout for all the cars featured in this book, unless the planned style for the 2.4 litre Standard model is included, and that never went into production. It is covered here in a period Jaguar Cars photograph, so no other mention will be made of it. In all cases the dashboards were built up at the factory as sub-structures and assembled into the car as units to be wired up to the main wiring loom.

Mk 1

The structure of the dashboard was made up of walnut veneer glued onto a hard wood substrate of numerous pieces. The centre section contained all the instruments and the majority of controls, and was supplemented at the sides by two glove box areas. A further wooden veneered panel formed the dashboard top rail as seen in the accompanying pictures, and this incorporated cut outs for the demister outlets. All these substrates were secured to the car's inner bulkhead area by a series of metal brackets, nuts, bolts and screws.

The driver's side glove box area did not have a lid, was finished internally in green baize. The outer veneered surround accommodated the chromed slider control with black plastic knob for the manual choke system on 2.4 litre models, or was blanked off with a chromed finisher for the 3.4 litre models which had an automatic choke system. The initial lettering on the choke plate was soon changed to match the font used on all other Jaguars of the time. On the passenger side the matching substrate included a veneered lid to the glove box, hinged from the bottom with two brass hinges secured by brass self-tapping screws. This lid had an external stained wooden knob, above which was a flush-mounted Wilmot Breedon chromed lock barrel. The glove box interior was finished in green baize to match the other side.

The main centre section of the dashboard was the same for both left and right hand drive models, and its layout of instruments and other switchgear was common to both 2.4 litre and 3.4 litre models. All instruments were supplied by Smiths Industries (except for the ammeter which came from

Lucas), and were mounted on a metal substrate behind the wood veneered panelling by nuts and bolts, the wood panelling forming merely a covering panel.

The instruments comprised a main 4¾-inch speedometer with black background, white legend and red tipped pointers. This was calibrated to 120mph (or the equivalent 190kph for some export markets), and incorporated the mileometer and odometer, with appropriate calibration settings for the axle ratio fitted to the car. Finally a small red tell-tale light at the centre base of the speedometer illuminated when the headlights' full beam was selected. The speedometer was fitted to the right-hand side of the dashboard, and on the left was a matching rev counter calibrated to 6000rpm, red lined from 5500rpm and incorporating an electric clock in the lower centre area.

The general layout of the Mk 1 dashboard applied to all models except the Standard – which would have had a centrally mounted speedometer and no rev counter if it had been produced.

This LHD Mk 1 shows the only dashboard difference to RHD examples, which is the location of the lockable glove compartment on the opposite side. The car has automatic transmission with its centrally mounted control.

The Mk 1 instrumentation followed the contemporary Jaguar practice in style, as seen in other models like the XK sports car. The only changes affected the rev counter range according to engine size. The large hole on the bottom right hand side is where a cigar lighter is fitted. Below that is the pull-out veneer capped ashtray. The two black knurled buttons (top left and right hand side) are screw-threaded and allow the whole central dashboard panel to be folded down to give access to wiring, lighting and fuses. This picture also shows the typical under-dash board covering, in vinyl trim to match the interior of the car and held in position by chromed screws with cup washers.

The auxiliary gauges all matched the style and colouring of the main instruments. The centrally mounted ammeter had simple C (charge) and D (discharge) markings, with two graduated sections each way. On the left was the fuel gauge, calibrated in quarters, and on the right an integrated oil pressure and water temperature gauge. The oil pressure section was calibrated in increments of 20 lb sq in and the lower temperature section in increments of degrees of from 30 to 100. This dual gauge was wired into capillary pipes to give readings direct from the engine.

Illumination for the instruments was typically 1950s Jaguar for the Mk 1 models, with small blue windows around the circumference of the instruments lit by four 2.2 watt bulbs.

The range of switchgear was all sited at the bottom of the veneered dash area, most of it in black plastic with appropriate naming and legends painted in white engraved into each control. Reading from left to right, the switches started with a large serrated circular control for wiper operation showing the 'off' and two speed positions, the switch having a twisting operation. Next came a smaller push button (with chrome surround ring) to switch on the heater fan, marked 'Fan'. To the right of that was a further push button of the same size, style and surround marked 'P' to operate the instrument panel illumination.

In the centre of the dashboard below and between the two main instruments there was the main lighting control switch. This had a matt black painted metal surround with

Situated on the dashboard top rail on the driver's side, this control operated the Jaguar Intermediate Speed hold on the automatic transmission or, on a manual gearbox model, it engaged overdrive on 4th gear. it was made from plastic and Bakelite; earlier examples had an illuminated Bakelite toggle switch.

the legend 'O' (off), 'S' (side), 'H' (head) and 'F' (fog) lights; the operating switch was made of chromed Mazak and had a knurled handle and pointer. Some export market cars did not have fog lights fitted, so a different surround without the 'F' position was used. Below this control there was a small chromed button with chrome surround to operate the vacuum windscreen washers and to the right a push button matching the panel switch, marked 'Int' and operating the interior lighting.

To the right of the dashboard were three more switches. First came the Wilmot Breeden chromed ignition switch with chromed surround, next an unmarked push button of the same style as the 'Int' and 'P' buttons to operate the starter, and finally to its right the Smiths cigarette lighter unit with a chromed surround and black plastic operating knob.

Below the central area main of the veneered dashboard there was a cross veneered finisher fillet and within that, below the ignition, starter and cigarette lighter switch group, there was a discreet pull-out ashtray with chromed interior and 'stub' area.

Where cars were equipped with automatic transmission, the operating control for this took the form of a blue-black Bakelite quadrant mounted to the lower dash area and bearing the legend 'P,N,D,L,R' above a matching lever that operated horizontally. Apart from an automatic transmission XK150, this was the only model of Jaguar using this system, which was a logical choice as its position suited both left- and right-hand-drive models. The same quadrant was also fitted to some other brands of cars at the time, such as Alvis.

Controls below and under the dash area comprised a control rod with shaped black plastic knob to open the scuttle ventilator and the knurled adjusters for the odometer and clock. These latter two were secured to board panelling covering the under-dash area by notched chrome escutcheons. The shaped boards were all covered in Rexine to match the car's interior colour scheme, glued appropriately and secured by chrome self-tapping screws through cup washers.

Other controls included the black plastic direction indicator stalk on the steering column surround. This was on the right

for right-hand-drive models and on the left for left-hand-drive cars. It was a simple three-position switch, with a self-cancelling cam controlled via the steering wheel position. The horn push was centrally mounted within the steering wheel boss. (For other information on the steering wheel area, please see the section on Steering elsewhere in this book).

Cars with overdrive or automatic transmission had a further switch mounted on the dashboard top rail in front of the driver. Initially of an illuminated Perspex type, this was changed from July 1958 to a conventional black plastic toggle switch without illumination. On overdrive cars it operated the overdrive solenoid and on automatic transmission models it operated the intermediate speed hold. (Both these subjects are covered in the Transmission section of this book.)

The rear view interior mirror was situated in two different positions according to model. On all early cars the mirror was mounted on a chromed stem on the centre of the dashboard top rail, the mirror itself being a simple rectangular convex type secured with clips. From September 1957 for 3.4 litre models, a more conventional roof-mounted mirror was fitted, with a metal backing in silver finish.

The headlight dimmer switch was operated by a Lucas

The Mk 1 switchgear, although not unique to these Jaguars, was unique to the 2.4 and 3.4 litre models. Made of black plastic with engraved legend in cream, the large black knob below the dash controls the scuttle ventilator. The chromed slider on the left controls the temperature of the heating.

The Mk 2 style of gear knob featured on all cars equipped with the Moss gearbox.

push-type switch fixed to the driver's side footwell by a U shaped bracket, the switch and bracket being in a dull zinc finish with a mushroom shaped black rubber cover. The pedal arrangement was conventional with three pendant pedals on manual cars or two on automatics. The brake and clutch pedals were finished in black paint and had black rubber pedal pads, with a 'crossed' grip pattern and a 'J' insignia.

Mk 2 and other models

A complete re-design of the interior took place with the introduction of the Mk 2 models in 1959 and the following remarks also apply to ALL other models, except where specifically stated.

The assembly and structure of the dashboard was very similar to the Mk 1s except that the centre section had all switchgear and auxiliary instruments directly attached in an easily accessible panel with no wood finishing. Also the main speedometer and rev counter were mounted directly onto the wooden substrate without the need for a metal mounting panel. Although there was still a glove box area on the passenger side, on the driver's side the main speedometer

Very early examples of the Mk 2 had the centre dash section painted in a matt black finish, and also had an oil pressure gauge reading to 100psi.

The more common later Mk 2 centre dash area with Rexine covered panel and a 60psi oil pressure gauge.

and rev counter took the place of another glove box. The dashboard top rail was now more substantial in size and shape, with cross-veneered fillets for the demister outlets and cross-banded veneer for the lower edge and top edge.

The passenger side glove box area had a veneered lid, hinged at the bottom with two chromed hinges secured by chromed self-tapping screws. The interior was again finished in green baize, but now had a blue plastic cover over the bulb illumination. This was operated by a black plastic switch in a chrome surround, activated when the glove box lid door was opened. Surprisingly, there was no longer a knob on the exterior to open the door; instead, the key had to be left in the Wilmot Breedon flush mounted lock and used as a handle.

The driver's side section of the dashboard now incorporated the matching speedometer and rev counter. These had a larger, 5-inch, diameter than their Mk 1 counterparts, with black painted metal bezels. Both were mounted on the wooden substrate via black rubber gaskets and secured in place by brackets and knurled nuts. Again made by Smiths, these instruments were much more substantial and detailed than before, with black backgrounds, a raised centre section, black and white tipped pointers, satin-finished centre mountings and white legends. The speedometer (on the right) was calibrated to 120mph on 2.4 litre and V8 models or to 140mph for the models with larger engines. Equivalent kph instruments were used where needed. The speedometer also incorporated the mileometer and odometer and its face carried the usual identification information. It also had three warning lights: blue for main beam headlights at the top, an amber coloured low fuel warning light at the bottom right, and a red ignition warning light.

The matching rev counter on the left was calibrated to 6000rpm, red lined from 5500rpm and incorporated a clock at the bottom centre. On Daimler V8-engined cars, the rev counters were red-lined from 6000rpm to 6500rpm.

It should be noted that although these instruments are of the same shape, size, fitting and style as those on many other Jaguar models, there are subtle differences because of gearing, calibration and even warning light/clock information.

On the same driver's panel, to the right of the speedometer were auxiliary switchgear and warning lights for a variety of purposes dependent on model, specification and year. All cars featured a large red light in the lower area which doubled as a handbrake on and low brake fluid warning; it was surrounded by a chromed screw escutcheon in a black plastic surround with the white painted legends 'Brake Fluid' and 'Handbrake'.

On 2.4 litre models and V8s, mounted vertically between the brake warning light and the speedometer was a manual choke slider control with a slightly bevelled shape and a black plastic control knob. Its painted metal legend panel was marked with 'Hot' 'Cold' and 'Off' positions. This was accompanied by a small red warning illumination bulb with chromed surround, centrally mounted above the slider control.

Above the brake warning light, cars fitted with a switchable heated rear screen had another switch. Here, the black panel with its white painted legend 'Rear Window' had a small red illuminated bulb with chrome surround on the left, and a push-pull chromed switch matching it on the right.

Yet another item found on cars fitted with the Borg Warner DG automatic transmission was a black toggle switch with black painted circular surround containing the white legend 'Intermediate Speed Hold'. This was on the dashboard top rail on the driver's side, and its function was to hold second gear when required.

This was the standard Mk 2 dashboard layout. The main instrumentation is in front of the driver and all auxiliary gauges and controls in a centrally mounted panel, which could be folded down for access to wiring, lighting and fuses.

This dash area to the right of the speedometer (on RHD cars) carries a red warning light that indicates either low brake fluid level or that the handbrake is on. The area above was used to fit auxiliary switches for items like the heated rear screen.

On 2.4 litre engine Mk 2s with a manual choke, the operating lever and warning bulb were featured next to the speedometer as shown here.

Speedometer and rev counter legends altered according to the engine fitted. These were for a 3.4 or 3.8 litre engine; the rev counter went up to 6,000rpm and was red-lined at 5,000rpm, while the speedometer was calibrated to 140mph.

The main centre section of the dashboard was the same for both LHD and RHD models, and contained the auxiliary gauges and other switchgear. Its layout was common to all models, with minor position exceptions. All instruments were again supplied by Smiths Industries except for the ammeter, which was made by Lucas. Like the switchgear, the gauges were mounted directly onto a metal substrate that formed the whole panel with no wood veneering; instead it was initially just painted matt black. From July 1960 this panel was fitted with a black Rexine textured covering glued to the unpainted metal. The substrate was hinged at its base and secured to the inner bulkhead area by two knurled metal threaded screws, one at each top corner of the panel, so that it could easily be folded down to access wiring, illumination and panel light bulbs.

There were four auxiliary gauges, which all matched the style, colouring and mounting of the main instruments. On the far left was the ammeter with simple C (charge) and D (discharge) markings and a graduated section each way. To the right of that was the fuel gauge calibrated in quarters. On the right of the lighting switch (see below), there was the oil pressure gauge. Initially calibrated to 100psi, it was changed to 60psi in January 1960 after complaints that readings looked low. To the right of that was the fourth gauge showing water temperature, calibrated in sections of degrees Centigrade marked 30 - 70 - 110. This later changed to a simplified gauge read out with a white (cool) band, a central 'normal' position and a red 'hot' mark (see Production Changes chapter). All instruments were internally illuminated by push fit bulbs from the rear of each unit.

In the centre between the two groups of auxiliary gauges was the main lighting control switch. This had a matt black painted plastic surround (flatter and simpler in design than on Mk 1s) with the legend 'O', 'S', 'H' and 'F'. (As before, 'F' was eliminated on cars not equipped with fog lamps). The switch also had the legend 'Lights' below it, and had a Mazak chromed operating lever with knurled handle and pointer as on the Mk 1.

The Daimler 2.5 litre V8 dashboard arrangement was virtually the same as that on a Mk 2. All Daimler V8 models had a manual choke, hence the same control lever on the right hand side. Veneering on the interior woodwork tended to be of a slightly higher quality than that used on most Jaguars.

Below the gauges was an array of six matching black plastic toggle switches fitted to the panel by notched chromed escutcheons. Again reading from left to right, on RHD cars these controlled interior lighting (two positions), panel lights (two positions with bright and dim positions), heater fan (two positions with slow and fast), map light, wipers (two positions with fast and slow) and washers (a single spring loaded position). These switch positions were reversed on LHD cars.

The six switches were grouped in two sections of three. The centre area between them was occupied by three non-matching switches. On the left was the Wilmot Breeden chromed ignition switch with chromed surround. In the centre was the Smiths cigarette lighter unit, smaller in diameter to that fitted to Mk 1s, with a chromed surround and black plastic operating knob. On the right was a black plastic starter push button, of a deeper style to that of the Mk 1 and common to all other 1960s Jaguars; this, too, had a chromed surround. For certain overseas markets and later for cars fitted with a steering lock in the UK, there were alternative arrangements. In some cases, the ignition barrel was changed to one containing an extra position to operate the starter, and in others the barrel was left disconnected and the Waso steering lock controlled the starter. In either case the black starter button was retained but not wired in.

The legends for the switches were marked in white on a black Perspex strip that was retained by four screws to the bottom of the folding centre dash panel. This strip was illuminated at night by the panel lights, and a thin piece of green plastic was sandwiched above the logo strip to alter the colour of the illumination.

As mentioned in the chapters on Transmissions and Steering, the steering column black plastic surrounds had a legend window on top used for a variety of notices. For all cars it featured green tell-tale arrows for the indicators. A white 'Overdrive' legend in the centre lit up when overdrive was engaged on cars so equipped; or, on automatic models,

The positioning of auxiliary switchgear like the heated rear screen altered from car to car, so the position on this Daimler is slightly different to that on the Mk 2 featured. There appears to be no logic in this!

On Daimler V8s, whether with manual or automatic transmission, the tunnel was carpeted and accommodated a single radio speaker facing the left-hand side of the car.

steering lock, and there were two different steering wheel designs. (Please see the Steering and Production Changes sections). Both designs featured a half horn ring in chrome.

As on the Mk 1 cars, below the dashboard centre section was a control for the scuttle ventilator. This consisted of a control rod with a flat black plastic knob with white engraved 'Vent' legend. There was also shallow storage area (ideal for a newspaper), covered in black baize with a full width veneered wooden finisher that had chromed edging finishers. Under the driver's dash area were the knurled adjusters for the odometer and clock, each one secured to the board panelling covering the under-dash area by notched chrome escutcheons. The shaped boards under both sides of the dashboard were all covered in Rexine to match the car's interior colour scheme, glued appropriately and secured by chrome self-tapping screws through cup washers.

The rear view interior mirror was always a conventional roof mounted type. Early cars, until mid-1960, featured the same type of mirror as used on other models like the Mark IX. This was a rectangular concave mirror within a strong metal surround with chrome edging strip and backing in gold paint, with a chromed stem and locking nut, a rubber stop between the mirror stem and windscreen to eliminate vibration and a chromed flat switch to control the anti-dazzle function. The later 1960 models and all subsequent ones used the standard Jaguar fit elongated mirror with a metal backing in polished grained silver finish with a plastic circular knob underneath to control the anti-dazzle function.

Headlight dipping was controlled by the same Lucas push-type switch and fittings as on the Mk 1 models. The pendant pedal arrangement was also initially like the Mk 1 type covered above, but from July 1960 the accelerator pedal was changed to an organ type.

the position of the automatic transmission stalk was indicated by a pointed on a 'P,N,D,L,R' readout (some later versions incorporated D1 and D2 positions). On post-1966 overdrive models, the illuminated word was replaced by a simple red bulb.

Chromed Mazak stalks mounted on the steering column and fitted with shaped black plastic tips were used to control the overdrive or automatic transmission gear selection operation and the indicators and headlamp flasher. In the beginning, the overdrive or automatic stalk was on the left and the indicator and flasher stalk was on the right, but by April 1960 the stalks had swapped sides and they continued that way throughout the rest of production for all the cars featured here.

The steering columns themselves changed little except for the adaptation to accept a Waso combination ignition and

A unique feature of the Daimler V8-250 model was this black vinyl covered dashboard top rail.

The centre console of these cars (please see the section on Interior) also incorporated some operational equipment. On its vertical face were the two slider controls for the heating and ventilation system; the sliders themselves had black legends (see Cooling section), and the control arms each had a black plastic knob. These sat alongside the area for a radio to be fitted. A radio was not a standard fit item, and usually there was a chromed Mazak blanking plate with a padded vinyl insert to match the interior trim. This plate was secured to the console from the rear by two chromed threaded studs with chromed nuts. Various radios were available as optional extras (please see the separate section in this book). Above the radio area was a rectangular speaker grille with a chromed rim and alloy mesh, of a standard design used by many other manufacturers. This was fitted even when the car had no radio.

Where the Mk 2 Jaguars had a centre console between the seats, the Daimler V8s did not. Instead, there was a much simpler metal arrangement with a wood veneered finish, hanging below the centre section of the dashboard.

The 240 and 340 models did not have such strong figuring to the veneered woodwork and lost the cross-banding on the edge of the top rail, which had been so prominent on earlier cars.

This 240/340 type of dashboard centre panel shows the later type of water temperature gauge. Later models were even fitted with a different battery condition indicator.

This was where the two slider controls for the heating and ventilation system were located. Again there was provision for a radio between them, that provision being covered by a wood veneer-covered blanking plate when no radio was fitted. Below the console was a pull-out ashtray of a standard contemporary design used by many other manufacturers. This had a chromed pull handle and no interior fitments, although the ashtray could be extracted by pressing the centre section when open.

The remaining areas below this console were carpeted over a board covering, into which was inserted a speaker grille of the size and type used on the Mk 2. For the few manual transmission V8s produced, the gear lever was positioned in the usual place with a black rubber gaiter surround secured around the carpet with clips. Because of this the gearbox cover extended upwards and was covered by carpet, eliminating the space for the speaker grille. In such cases a large circular speaker grille was positioned to the left hand side; it had an alloy finished mesh within a black metal surround.

S-type models

There was no need for a complete re-design of the interior from Mk 2 to S-type, but there are many subtle differences covered here, some of which also applied to the 420 and Sovereign. The unique features of those two models are covered later in this chapter.

The dashboard top rail for the S-type is not interchangeable with its Mk 2 equivalent. Although it was the same in style and build, it is subtly different in shape with chromed finishers at each end. All three of the dashboard sections were again of the same build and assembly and contain many of the features of the Mk 2 but were of a different design. The outer sections (glove box and main instrumentation areas) were more upright and lost the scalloped sections at the base, but gained curved corners.

The passenger side glove box door was smaller and now incorporated a chromed pull handle below the lock barrel, attached by two chromed self-tapping screws from the inside. The driver's side section that incorporated the main instruments and some of the switchgear had exactly the same layout as the Mk 2, except that the wood panel was sculpted out, allowing the speedometer and rev counter to sit 'in' rather than 'on' the panel.

The main centre section of the dashboard was now a proper wood veneered panel, although it contained the same equipment and was hinged in the same way as on the Mk 2. The other differences were that the auxiliary gauges were inset into the woodwork like the speedometer and rev counter, while the row of toggle switches was now in an inset black Ambla covered section. The Perspex legend strip to illustrate the operation of the toggle switches changed because S-types (like 420s and Sovereigns) had twin fuel tanks. The switch controlling the interior lights now had two positions and operated the map light as well, while the old map light switch position was now occupied by a fuel tank changeover switch. The legends changed accordingly. Also underneath the centre dash panel, there was a wood-veneered pull-out tray with a chromed handle like that fitted to the glove box door.

The area below the dash was now totally different. It had a full-width parcel shelf with curved ends where it met the door areas; the edges were trimmed in leather to match the interior trim and the shelf had a black baize covering. The centre area formed the top of the centre console and transmission tunnel which was also of a different design to that of the Mk 2 and V8s.

On either side, a wood veneered shaped section continued where the leather edging left off, and in the centre was a chromed area with the heater controls. These consisted of two knurled chromed knobs to control air distribution and a central horizontal chrome slider with black knob to control

The dashboard layout for the S-type model followed the same design format as the Mk 2, with some enhancements. The veneered wood sections for the glove box and driver's side instrumentation were now more shapely with rounded edges, and they lost the sculpted bottom sections to make room for a full-width parcel shelf. The glove box was now fitted with a chromed handle and it was no longer necessary to use a key to gain access to the interior.

The centre panel for auxiliary instruments and switches was wood veneered to match the rest of the dashboard on the S-type, and the gauges were slightly inset into the wooden panel. There was also a neat pull-out veneered tray with a chromed handle to match that of the glove box.

the temperature; this had the legends 'Hot' and 'Cold' painted in white on a black background. There was no need for a manual control to operate the scuttle ventilator as on the Mk 2, because the S-types had the Mark X's sophisticated vacuum operated system.

A wood-veneered hardwood insert panel was bolted to the vertical face of the centre console, and this was exactly the same as the one fitted to the contemporary 'big brother' Mark X saloon. This panel contained the same push-button air and heater control system, with three black plastic buttons labelled (from left to right) 'Air', 'Heat' and 'Off'. Above this switch pack was a rectangular wood-veneered ashtray, its stained rectangular 'pull' glued in place. The ashtray contained a chromed insert which was removable. Above all this was inset a mesh alloy finished grille, which acted as a blanking plate if a radio was not fitted. When a radio was fitted, it was mounted in a black Ambla covered panel.

The rest of the centre console had the same structure as the Mk 2, but was very different, with a more sculpted shape and style, extra padding and a more luxurious look. As on the Mk 2, it incorporated the manual transmission gear lever, but it also had a black plastic switch which controlled the flow of air to the rear compartment. The legends on this switch – 'Rear', 'Vent', 'On' and 'Off' – were engraved and painted

The centre console came in for a re-design with the S-type, not just to enhance the overall ambience of this up-rated model but also to accommodate the revised heating and ventilating system. Following the design of the Mark X models, the wood veneered panelling inset into the console trim incorporated three black plastic push buttons for on/ off, heat and air controls, the latter operated by vacuum. A separate black switch set into the console itself opened and closed a valve to the rear compartment. Nicely inset into the roll of the parcel shelf were the chromed circular controls and slider for heater and air direction. Incorporated into the vertical wood panel was also the cut-out for the radio and a pull-out veneered ashtray.

On this S-type main instrument panel, note the fitment of the intermediate speed hold switch on the right for the automatic transmission.

white. To the sides of the tunnel were two silver mesh circular grilles with chrome surrounds, one of which was for the radio speaker, the other a dummy used for aesthetic reasons. As with the Daimler V8s, because of the type of front seating the centre console did not continue to the rear of the car.

As already explained in the section on Steering, S-type models were only ever fitted with the later Mark X style steering wheel with the central circular push button.

420 and Sovereign models

With the introduction of the 420 and Sovereign models, Jaguar made more changes to the dashboard layout.

The wood veneered dashboard top rail disappeared entirely to be replaced by a more substantial black-trimmed surround panel made of pre-formed foam which formed the top rail, the corner surrounds and the bottom of the dashboard area as well. Centrally mounted on the top was an area for the new style square electrically driven clock (a spin-off from the one fitted to the 420G model). This incorporated a black metal painted surround and a black painted background, and both the hands and the legend on the face were white.

Although basically of the same dimensions and size, the veneered wooden substrates of the dashboard were new, following the general line of the S-type but inset into the 420

The dashboard layout of the Jaguar 420 and Daimler Sovereign is another variation of the original Mk 2 theme, and again different to that used on the S-type model. The whole of the wooden dashboard area was encased into a black vinyl covered pre-formed surround which necessitated new wooden panelling, all flush mounted. This allowed Jaguar to accommodate a deeper full width parcel shelf, with a black vinyl covered roll edge.

Prominently positioned in the padded dashboard top rail was a rectangular clock, a straight lift from the larger 420G in the Jaguar saloon range. This meant that a revised rev counter without the integrated clock was needed. With the advent of this new style of dashboard for the 420 and Sovereign models, the interior layout no longer had a pull-out tray of the type fitted to S-type models.

foam surround, held in place by nuts onto the captive bolts in the foam.

The passenger side glove box door was now slightly smaller and of a different shape to the S-type to match the curvature of the foam surround at that end of the dashboard. The driver's side was similarly treated and contained the instrumentation and switchgear (as on Mk 2s and S-types) according to specification. A difference was that the rev counter, otherwise of the same design, did not incorporate a clock. It was also re-calibrated to only 5500rpm, red lined from 5000rpm.

The main centre section of the dashboard was also incorporated into the foam surround, with its own matching bottom section screwed to the underside of the panel below the Perspex legend strip. Instrumentation was as before except that all 420 and Sovereign models had the later type of water temperature gauge (see the Mk 2 section). The below dash area and centre console followed the same style as the S-type, but the 420 and Sovereign models did not have the S-type's wood-veneered pull-out occasional tray with its chromed handle.

Like the S-types, 420s and Sovereigns were only ever fitted with the later Mark X style steering wheel with its centrally mounted horn push button.

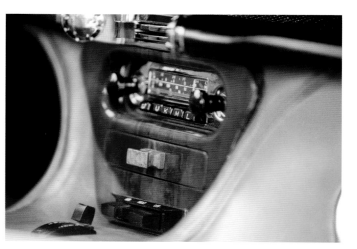

Although the controls are the same as the S-type, the veneered wooden plinth on the 420 and Sovereign is actually a different shape.

Unlike all the other models, the S-type and 420 featured two chromed radio speaker grilles, one each side of the centre console. However only one had a speaker, the other was a dummy.

INTERIOR TRIM AND BOOT INTERIOR

There are two distinctly different interior trim approaches to the cars featured in this book. The very traditional features of the Mk 1 range echo those of Jaguar throughout the 1950s, whereas once the Mk 2 was introduced the interior trim took on a new brightness that followed through to all other Jaguar models of the 1960s. As with earlier chapters, therefore, this one is split into features of the Mk 1 range and Mk 2, with differences for the Daimlers, S-types, 420 and Sovereign covered independently where necessary.

MK 1 CARS

Seating

Common features of both 2.4 and 3.4 litre models were that there was a single bench-type rear seat arrangement with a centre armrest and individual front seats of two different styles. Front seat frames were bolted in four places through captive nuts in the floorpan, were always finished in grey paint and had a fore and aft rail adjustment by means of a lever and spring system.

All seat facings were upholstered in Connolly Vymura leather with Vynide sides and other trim onto Dunlopillo foam cushioning, underneath which was a sprung package in untreated metal. Piping was always of the same colour as the main trim (unless by very special order at the time), and the trim was stretched over the foam areas and secured to framing hidden underneath the seat by means of black metal spring clips.

Manual-transmission cars had two bucket-style front seats with no side supports or armrests. There were seven vertical pleats to both the seat squab and backrest, and the backs of the seats were made up from shaped board panels, upholstered and attached to the main seat area. At the base of the rear of the front seats, cut-outs left space for rear seat passengers' feet and the seat bases were finished in moquette dyed to match the interior trim. Seat backs were not adjustable, and were never fitted with a reclining mechanism.

On models with automatic transmission equipped models (and as an option for manual transmission cars) a split front bench type arrangement was fitted. Both seats were still entirely separate with their own frames. With much flatter facings and again with no bolsters to give lateral support, the seats met in the middle and were trimmed accordingly to look like a continuous bench. Each squab and backrest had 11 vertical pleats, and although they used a different shape of frame, these cars still featured the same rails and type of adjustment. Front seat backs were plainer but of the same assembly, although there was no moquette finishing at the bottom; the vinyl panelling curved round to meet the seat sides and also finished higher up, eliminating the need for cut-out areas.

The rear seat for all these cars was of the same style, a single bench arrangement with 25 vertical pleats in the base and 11 pleats per side in the backrest. It had a single centrally mounted pull-down armrest, which just met the horizontal piping between the pleating and the front section of unpleated leather when in the down position. The front of the armrest

The front interior of the 2.4 litre (Mk 1) saloon with bucket seats fitted to manual transmission 2.4 and 3.4 litre cars. The carpet had a sewn-in heel pad, as depicted here.

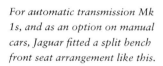

For automatic transmission Mk 1s, and as an option on manual cars, Jaguar fitted a split bench front seat arrangement like this.

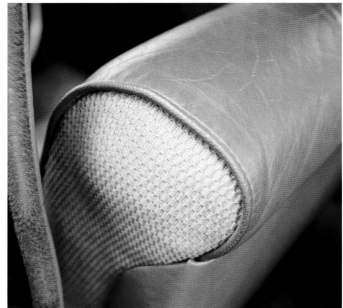

Side panel finish on the bench seats was very different in this cross-hatch vinyl material.

incorporated a looped finger pull in leather, long enough to remain visible when the armrest was in the closed position within the backrest. Mk 1 rear seats were trimmed at the top with two separate pieces of leather, so there was a join with double stitching right in the middle of the seat back.

The seat cushion and backrest were made up in the same way as the front seats. The cushion was a single unit which merely clipped into position. The backrest was clipped over the top of the bulkhead near the rear parcel shelf area and bolted to the rear bulkhead at two points in the base via black metal brackets area.

The rear parcel shelf was a wooden substrate with padded foam vinyl trim to match the rest of the interior, glued and spring-clipped in position.

Other Trim

Door trims were the same for all models and had a quite simple design, upholstered in Vynide with no piping or pre-forming. The upholstery was foam backed and glued to a plywood board frame secured by black spring clips around the edges and stapled where necessary. At the base of each door trim there were rectangular flat pockets similarly upholstered, the

Rear seating accommodation for the 2.4 and 3.4 litre Mk 1 models was visually slightly different to later cars (see other pictures). This picture also shows the different style to the backs of the individual front seats compared to the bench arrangement – they were finished with a moquette treatment at the bottom.

The backrest top leather panel on Mk 1 models was made from two separate pieces of leather, stitched in the middle.

Sun visors were treated differently according to model. The Mk 1s all had this type of soft-finish visor with chrome trim and swivel hinges.

Unique to the Mk 1 models were the wood surrounds to the window frames.

ones at the front having a slightly greater depth with a degree of springiness through the two webbing straps fitted internally to match the trim colour.

All doors were fitted with similarly upholstered armrests of different sizes and styles front and rear, bolted through to the door cards. Veneered walnut hardwood cappings were fitted to all doors, screwed with self-tappers through to the door frame. As the doors incorporated metal window frames, these areas were also fitted with wood veneered surrounds, spring-clipped into place through holes pre-drilled in the metal frame.

All four doors featured opening quarter-lights with conventional chromed handles and hinges taken from Wilmot Breeden stock items.

Vynide was also used either directly glued or mounted on board in other areas like the B/C post trims, clipped to the bodyshell by black metal clips through appropriately drilled holes. This also applied to the front compartment kick panel areas in the footwells and to the finisher areas between the back seat and rear wheelarch and door areas. The rear seat pan (below the actual seat cushion) was also upholstered in vinyl, glued to cover all exposed metal areas.

Door furniture was made up of matching chromed Mazak door handles and window winders held in place by cotter pins through holes in chromed escutcheons. Although these handles could be mounted in numerous ways, the correct position for the front doors is for the door handle to be facing downwards and the window winder to be at the four o'clock position; for the rear doors, the handle should face upwards and the winder should be at the two o'clock position.

Headling

Headlinings were of a wool cloth mix finished in a choice of grey or light beige (occasionally green if a green interior was specified). They were secured in position by transverse bars.

Two sun visors were standard equipment, both finished in the same trim as the headlining. Each had a chromed trim surround to three sides for protection against damage to the trim, and this also provided a neat way of 'sealing' the wool cloth. Internally made of flexible board, they were hinged on two chromed trim clips, one each side. The passenger side visor had a vanity mirror glued to the underside. Green Perspex visors were an optional extra.

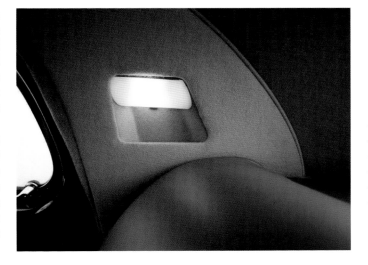

Interior lighting for the Mk 1 saloons followed style used in the contemporary Mark VII to IX saloons, with one lamp per side set into the headlining between the D post and the rear screen. The small chromed clip seen below the plastic shade allowed it to be released to change the bulb.

The style of the rear door trim style on the Mk 1s was similar to that of the front doors, but there was a different pocket arrangement and an elongated armrest matched the shaping of the rear seat cushion. On this example the door handle is incorrectly fitted; it should be pointing down, as in the picture to the left.

Door trims for both the 2.4 and 3.4 litre Mk 1 followed exactly the same design. They incorporated a solidly mounted armrest and a stretch map pocket, all finished in vinyl.

There was a different carpeting arrangement for automatic transmission and LHD Mk 1 models.

Carpets

The carpets were produced from close loop-pile Wilton with leather edging dyed and stitched to match the carpet colour. They came in various individual sections which were laid flat onto an underfelt. On the driver's side there was a Hardura coated area to match the rectangular heel pad stitched into the carpet. In some cars this was actually replicated on the passenger's side, but there is no record of this being a special order feature. Possibly the reason for this anomaly was simply availability on the assembly lines of carpets for both LHD and RHD models.

Door seals and trim

There were no seals attached to the actual door frames. Instead a flat black rubber seal was glued into a metal channel around the frames. In addition, Furflex trim matched to the interior colour scheme was pinned around on the inside of the door frame areas.

Sill treadplates were fitted to all models. Made of pressed aluminium with a cross-hatched design, they were shaped to fit on top of the Furflex trim on the inside of each door frame and sill area, lying flat on top of the painted sill inner face and with holes in securing vertical extensions through which rivets secured them to the sill. This area of attachment was hidden by the bottom section of the rubber door seals on the sill area.

Boot interior

Boot interiors were the same for all Mk 1s, quite plainly finished in body colour with little additional trim.

The boot sides were covered in a shaped millboard painted to a light grey finish, secured to the bodywork by chromed self-tapping screws with cup washers. Within the left-hand side rear wing area, the SU fuel pump and wiring were mounted to the bodyshell on two rubber bobbins. Because of this the board on that side had a pronounced circular bulge.

The boot floor had a shaped Hardura matting in dark grey with hessian backing and stitched vinyl edging. The wheelarch areas, boot floor and rear bulkhead were left in body-coloured painted metal. The boot floor had a plain black metal access panel set into the left-hand side to give access to the fuel tank sender unit.

A large ribbed access panel or lid in the boot floor gave

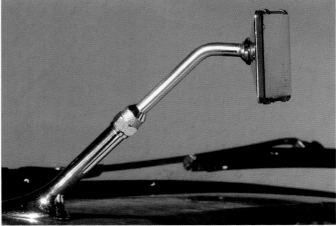

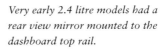

Very early 2.4 litre models had a rear view mirror mounted to the dashboard top rail.

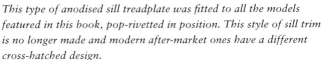

This type of anodised sill treadplate was fitted to all the models featured in this book, pop-rivetted in position. This style of sill trim is no longer made and modern after-market ones have a different cross-hatched design.

access to the spare wheel well, similarly ribbed and painted in body colour. The lid had a welded flat handle area at the front and the underside was suitably strengthened with longitudinal supports. A square black rubber (later foam) wedge was glued to the underside centre area of the lid to butt up against the fitted tool kit and prevent it from moving around in transit.

In the spare wheel well, a drainage hole was provided to release any water that accumulated, and was fitted with a black circular rubber bung. The well was deep enough to fit a spare wheel even of the wire spoked type. Wheels were stored upside down with the inner hub face secured by a large black screw and

pressed metal bracket, screwing through to a welded threaded support in the centre of the floor.

A comprehensive tool kit was fitted to all models – although the elusive Standard 2.4 litre model was not to have one! The kit came in a metal casing painted in gloss black, shaped to fit the inside of the spare wheel and with a pre-formed green baize interior which had cut-outs to accept a comprehensive range of tools. (The list of these appears elsewhere in this book.) The metal casing had a hinged lid, and the lid itself had a foam insert to prevent the tools from moving or rattling.

The two larger tools required, a jack and a combined wheelbrace and jack handle, were accommodated at the rear of the boot. The jack was on the bulkhead, and the handle on the underside of the parcel shelf area; both were held in place by unpainted metal spring clips.

The boot trim and layout remained virtually the same throughout Mk 1 and Mk 2/ Daimler V8 production. A simple Hardura matting in grey was stud-fitted to the boot floor, and board panelling was secured to the right-hand side to cover the inner wing area. Fixings were chromed screws with cup washers, and on the left-hand side the panel incorporated a dome shape to cover an inner wing area that also incorporated the fuel pump, piping and fuel filler.

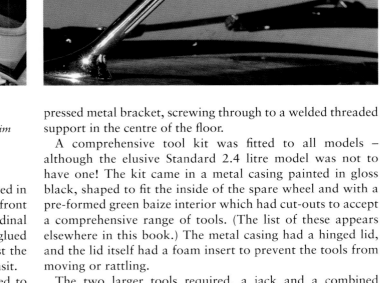

This shows the underside of the Hardura boot mat, with all the body panelling painted in the exterior finish. The large circular cover lifts up to reveal the spare wheel and tool kit. The black painted metal circular cover on the left gives access to the fuel tank gauge sender unit.

The styling of the front interior on Mk 2 saloons remained constant through production. This car belonging to David Rogers features the extra-cost Reutter reclining front seats; note the handle down by the handbrake and the extra flocked finisher panel to hide the mechanism.

This was the rear seating arrangement in all Mk 2 models, the front seat backs incorporating fold-down upholstery picnic tables.

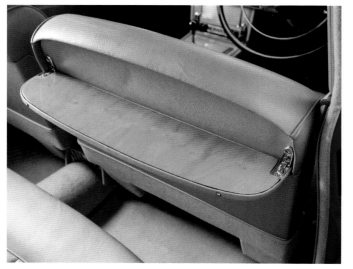

The fold-down picnic tables fitted to the majority of Mk 2s. The tables were held in the closed position by two spring-loaded balls, as shown here. This changed to a single, centrally mounted ball retainer in 1960.

Mk 2 cars

As a result of the significant differences between the Mk 1 and Mk 2 interiors, very little was carried over from one model to the other.

Seating

The majority of the seating for the Jaguar Mk 2 range was unchanged in design through the period of production, except for items mentioned below and the change from leather to Ambla upholstery in September 1966. The general structure, frame and fixings were the same as on the bucket-seat Mk 1 range, although the upholstery design was totally different.

The front seating had less shaping to that of the Mk 1. It was still upholstered in leather, initially with seven vertical pleats, but from about mid-1960 with eight pleats and with extra piping stitched horizontally along the sides and terminating at the front. Fillet shaped panels made of board, upholstered with moquette glued to them, were fitted to the seat sides to hide the space between the cushion and the seat back. On cars fitted with the optional extra reclining seats, this area was different (please see later section in this book).

The seat back was made up in the same way as the Mk 1 but differently shaped; the panelling folded around to the side of the seat, and at the bottom there was a moquette finished trim as before. Cut-away areas were built into the moquette area but these were found to be too small and were extended from March 1963 to allow more space for occupants' feet.

The seat backs incorporated fold-down occasional tables sculpted to the shape of the top of the seats, each one hinged at the bottom by two small chromed hinges, one each side and hidden when the tables were in the closed position. Initially the tables were secured shut by two chromed spring-loaded balls in the lid that located in the top of the seat back. Later in 1960 this was changed to a single ball in a surround, centrally mounted, that located in the seat back. The inside of the tables were fitted with a hard wood, straight grained

Rear passenger legroom was never a strong point of the Mk 2 and later ranges. The slimmer seat backs of the Mk 1 models were less of a problem in this respect. The very early Mk 2 cars had a smaller cutout at their base to help with legroom; it was covered in a single piece of moquette. Later cars like this one had an extended cutout with separate panels and moquette covering.

veneered panel to form the tray area. A chromed pull handle was mounted on the exterior of the upholstered face of the table. These picnic tables were deleted with the changeover to Ambla upholstery from September 1966.

The rear seat for the Mk 2 had the same style and assembly as its Mk 1 equivalent, although the shaping of the seat cushion was very subtly different with a wider plain section between the piped pleated area and the front of the seat. Also the seat back top was now upholstered from a single piece of leather, so eliminating the need for the centrally stitched area.

A major change took place in September 1966 when Ambla (plastic) upholstery replaced leather on all models except the Daimler V8s. Leather however remained available as an extra cost option if required. As already mentioned, the occasional tables were deleted when this change took place.

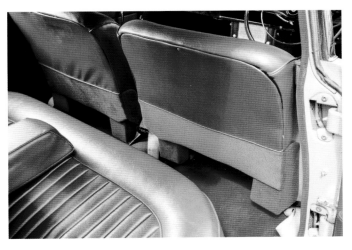

Ambla (plastic) trim replaced leather as the standard fit on very late Mk 2s, 240 and 340 models. It brought some very subtle changes to the styling and stitching, as in this 240 owned by Jaguar Heritage

This later type of seat back without picnic tables was fitted to the very last of the Mk 2s and then all 240 and 340 models.

89

Mark 2 rear door trim treatment with solid storage pocket, armrest incorporating ashtray and horizontal pleating to match the front door trims. Note that all doors now have chromed window frames with no wood surrounds.

Mk 2 front door trim with spring-loaded pocket, new styled armrest and horizontal pleating to the vinyl trim panel.

Other Trim

The structure and finish of the door trims on Mk 2s was the same as on Mk 1s, but their style was different. Front and back trims now incorporated two heat-formed seams running horizontally front to rear of the panels. The armrests were also of a totally different style and although the front door pockets operated the same way as before, they too were of a different style and shape (see accompanying pictures). The rear door pockets had a solid structure, allowing for larger items to be stowed. Again they had restyled armrests, now incorporating a contemporary chromed square ashtray with slide-open lid.

Wood veneered trim was also different. Similar but differently shaped door top cappings were fitted and secured in the same way, but now with an additional flat fillet of plain stained wood as a finisher to each door top, secured in place by chromed self-tapping screws with chromed cup washers.

Unlike the Mk 1s, the Mk 2s had separate window frames

which were bolted down into the door structure. These were made of brass and chromed, and there was no need for additional wood trim around them. In November 1960 the frames had strengthening sections added at their bases, and because of this the stained wood fillet had to be cut out

The centre console arrangement common to all Jaguar Mk 2 models incorporated a lidded ashtray. Note the blanking panel fitted by Jaguar when a radio was not incorporated. Finished in vinyl, the cast chromed surround was attached to the console by two screws and nuts.

Wood door cappings for the Mk 2, 2.5 litre V8 and S-type were in two parts, the lower vertical section in veneer screwed to the door frame and an upper horizontal thin stained wooden strip held to the lower wooden section by chromed domed screws with chromed cup washers. Due to the early identification of stress cracks in the chrome-on-brass window frames, all later cars were fitted with this vertical strengthener at the base of the frame.

accordingly to accommodate them. These chromed window frames were further modified in April 1963 to accommodate flocked rubber channel inserts.

As before there were four opening quarter-light windows, now part of the separate window frame structure. The rear ones now followed the design used by Jaguar on the Mark V to IX models and which would become common to other Jaguar saloons up to the introduction of the XJ6. A lever in chromed Mazak swivelled to open the hinged quarter-light to various degrees and incorporated a 'stop'.

Centre console

On the Mk 2, the console was secured below the dashboard central area by a large chromium plated knurled knob on each side, and at the rear between the front seats by another knob. The console continued vertically down and then horizontally rearwards between the two front seats, covering the front middle area of the transmission tunnel completely. Inside it would be found the twin black convoluted hoses taking air from the heater ducts under the dashboard to the plated grille for the rear seat passengers.

The console itself was made of metal and covered in leather to match the interior trim, with piping each side and a flocked area at the rear. As well as the exit for the manual transmission gear lever with leather gaiter (which on early cars had a chromed collar), there was also an ash tray with its lid trimmed in leather to match the console and fitted with a Jaguar growler plastic badge. The lid had a full width piano hinge in chrome finish at the rear, secured by chromed self-tapping screws. Internally the ashtray lid was covered in black baize and the base of the ashtray itself was fitted out in chrome with a detachable tray. There was also a neat leather 'pull' to the lid. Early cars did not have a lid support arm, which was added late in 1960.

Common to all Mk 2, 240, 340, Daimler, S-type and 420 models was this style of roof-mounted rear view mirror.

Headlining

The headlining on all UK-built Mk 2s was of the same type and style as the Mk 1 equivalent, but local content requirements in some cars assembled overseas from CKD dictated the use of fabric or plastic headlinings. The two sun visors were initially different, being recessed into the headlining, but then the Mk 1 style was adopted and remained the norm through to the end of production. The earlier style of visor took their cue from those used in the Mark VII to IX models. They had a stiff board substrate, were rectangular in shape with squared edges, and were upholstered with woollen cloth. They also had a centre cut-out to accept the chromed pull handle and holder for a circular black rubber securing tab that connected into a chromed clip in the headlining. The headlining itself was cut out with a recessed upholstered area to accept each sun visor so it would lie flat when closed on those early cars. The visor was secured via two complex chromed hinges, one each side.

Headlining manufacture, fitting and sun visors were standardised with those of the S-type model from September 1966.

Although looking the same as those fitted to the Mk 1, the later Mk 2 style sun visors have a subtly different shape. The fittings are the same.

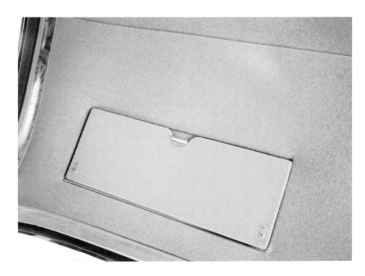

The very early Mk 2 models featured this type of inset solid sun visor akin to that fitted to the Mark VII to IX models of the period.

Carpets

The carpets were produced from closer smoother pile Wilton with leather edging dyed and stitched to match the carpet colour. The same principles applied, in that different pieces of carpet were glued, held loosely or held by bow fasteners (which were replaced in March 1964 by stud fasteners). Areas such as underneath the centre console were not fully carpeted. Starting in September 1966, the carpets were progressively changed over the years, first with a thinner tufted type of material, and then moving over to very thin nylon carpeting that was not as durable.

Some pieces of carpet were replaced by a single front floor and toeboard carpet in May 1964. In July 1967, Velcro nylon strip carpet fasteners were applied to all carpets.

Door seals

From August 1961, all cars were fitted with extra black rubber seals in the channel to the leading edge of the front doors. In September 1966, the door window frames were revised with rubber seals replacing weather strips.

Boot

The comprehensive tool kit remained pretty much the same for most of production, although the metal case did change to one made of black plastic (please see the Tools and Handbook section for full details).

DAIMLER V8s

Seating

Front seating for the V8s was very different, with what might be called a retrospective style like that used in the split-bench arrangement in the Mk 1s. The front seats were still individual but formed a split-bench arrangement, and included individual fold-down armrests in the centre, with chrome hinged mechanisms and leather pull eyes. The seats in the 'wide bumper' models had a total of 11 vertical pleats in the cushions and eight in the seat backs. Those in the later 'slim line' bumper cars (from September 1967) used different perforated leather for the pleating, with a total of 17 pleats in the cushion and 16 in the backrest.

Moquette covered boards were used as fillets on the seat sides to hide the gap between the cushion and backrest, similar to those on the Mk 2 but of a different shape. The seat frames and adjustment used the same mechanism as the Mk 2s.

Despite the fact that Daimlers were more expensive than the equivalent Jaguar and were considered of a slightly higher status, the backs of the front seats did not accommodate occasional tables. Nor did they have any other special adornment, but were just upholstered with a simple moulded area following the contour of the seat and with the usual moquette-finished bottom section incorporating cut-outs for the passengers' feet.

Although not substantially different to that of the Jaguar models, the interior of the Daimler V8s was quite subtly changed in many ways. This general interior view of a Daimler 2.5 litre V8 owned by the Jaguar Heritage Trust shows the most obvious difference, which is the front seating arrangement. It is a split-bench type, similar but not the same as the styling of the equivalent Mk 1s. These seats were always finished in leather incorporating neat fold-away armrests in the centre. The main carpeting areas were the same as on the Mk 2 models except for the transmission tunnel area where there was no centre console.

As the Daimler V8 seats were of a different design and thinner than the Mk 2 type, no picnic tables were built in.

The rear seating area of the Daimler V8 models. With the thinner backed front seats, legroom was marginally better.

The twin front seat armrests of the Daimler V8 models.

From September 1967, reclining seats were standardised on Daimler V8 models, operated by a chromed Mazak lever on the door side of each front seat. This necessitated a change to the seat frame accordingly, as return springs were incorporated.

The rear seat followed Mk 2 practice except that on the later models with 'slim line' bumpers the perforated pleating as seen on the front seats was duplicated with 42 pleats in the cushion and 14 per side in the backrest. As at the front, in September 1967 ventilated pleating was standardised on V8-250 models.

Other Trim

Although the structure and finish of the door trims followed the same principle as on contemporary Jaguars, and in this case the actual board and upholstery were the same, detail changes were made to the armrests and pockets. For the 'wide bumper' models, the door pocket in the front door was of the same shape and style as fitted to the Mk 1s, while the front door armrest was neater, effectively just the top padded section of the Mk 2's armrest without the extra shaped trimming underneath. For the rear doors the same approach applied. This time a full-width door pocket was accompanied by a styled armrest around it, once again containing an ashtray.

With the introduction of the V8-250, the door trims were

When manual transmission was specified on the Daimler V8-250 models, a conventional rubber gaiter surround was fitted into the carpet area.

Interior door trims were simplified with the introduction of the Daimler V8-250 model. Now with the single strip of stained wood finisher (like the earlier model, pictured right), the veneered capping was replaced by a padded upholstered panel similar to that fitted to later Jaguar models like the 420.

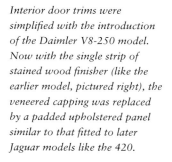

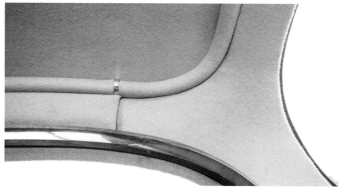

Interior door trims (front, to the left, and rear, above) were styled differently for the Daimler V8 models, even down to the pocket area.

Daimler V8 models only had a single rear compartment courtesy light fitted in the centre of the headlining above the rear screen.

The headlining style and fitment was different for the Daimler V8 models, as depicted here.

The front interior area of the S-type shows the most marked difference between this and the other models, which was the seating arrangement. Its styling and design continued for the 420 and Sovereign models. Front seat armrest design followed that of the Daimler V8 seats. Most S-types were upholstered in leather but a few of the last cars produced had Ambla trim.

subtly altered and there were changes to the wood veneer furniture on the doors as well. Out went the deep veneered cappings and in came a padded, upholstered roll attached with spring clips to the door panel and frame. To finish this off, a flat wood stained fillet (like the one previously used) was applied to the top, retained in the same way as on the earlier cars.

Headlining

Headlining was the same as in other models, except that from the introduction of the V8-250 the company adopted a single-piece padded woollen cloth lining that did not require any internal supports, but was instead glued to the roof. This incorporated a padded and wood-covered roll around the outer rim.

S-TYPE, 420 AND SOVEREIGN MODELS

The following notes are applicable to both the S-type and the 420 and Sovereign models as well, except where indicated.

Seating

Another more modern style of front seat was used on the S-type, 420 and Sovereign models. It was something of a cross between the split-bench style of the Mk 1 and Daimler V8s and that of the Mk 2. These seats had wider cushions and incorporated a curved approach to the plain leather area at the front and the pleated area in the centre of the seat. They were also upholstered from smaller pieces of leather stitched together.

On the S-type, the pleats were in plain leather, but the 420 and Sovereign had a total of 16 perforated pleats in each cushion, with a larger plain section either side stitched at

both ends. S-type, 420 and Sovereign seats also incorporated individual armrests in the same size and style as those used in the Daimler V8s. The seat backs were also quite thin and again followed the same profile, size and trim as the Daimlers. Even though these were more expensive 'up-market' models, there were again no occasional tables, but at least the thinner seat backs provided a little extra legroom in the rear compartment, and a reclining mechanism was standard specification on all these models. The 420 and

The rear compartment of the S-type models, with simple front seat backs, also featured in the 420 and Sovereign models.

Rear seat design for the S-type, 420 and Sovereign displays a shallower rake to the rear seat back for improved headroom.

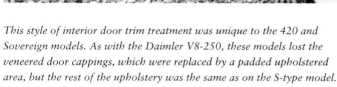

This style of interior door trim treatment was unique to the 420 and Sovereign models. As with the Daimler V8-250, these models lost the veneered door cappings, which were replaced by a padded upholstered area, but the rest of the upholstery was the same as on the S-type model.

Sovereign had perforated leather pleats on the rear seat to match those on the front seats.

The seat fore and aft adjustment was different to the Mk 1 and Mk 2, in that instead of the conventional sliding runners, these models used swinging links that lowered the front of the seats and raised the rear as the seats were moved progressively forward.

The rear seat followed the same styling treatment as the front but with a much more shapely backrest. To create more space in the rear compartment, the rear squab was 2 inches (50mm) thinner than that of the Mk 2, with a more steeply

This picture shows front and side detail of the headlining style and fitment in the Daimlers, S-types and 420s.

inclined backrest. With 20 pleats per side in the cushion and a centre plain area, and 17 pleats per side in the backrest, there was the obligatory fold down centre armrest, but this time much wider in profile and shorter in length than before. As with the front seating, the 420 and Sovereign models used perforated leather.

Other Trim

Yet another change to the door trims came in for the S-type. Looking much plusher, each upholstered door card incorporated two sets of four pre-welded seams running horizontally the full width of the doors. At the top, the doors retained the full wood veneered treatment of the Mk 2s, and a roll of upholstery finished off the door trim to meet the wood. Door handles and window winders were unchanged from Mk 2 types.

The 420 and Sovereign models differed here as they adopted the same styling approach for the top of the door trims as the V8-250, without the solid wood veneer but with the flat wood stained fillet.

The front doors had a new style of solid armrest, still upholstered but secured from underneath by screws into the door card via chrome trimmed holes. This was very much in the style of those fitted to the Mark X and 420G saloons. The rectangular door pocket was now also much plusher with a chromed 'pull'. There was a new door locking mechanism, and the handle no longer had to be pushed forward to lock the door from the inside; instead there was a chromed

A larger boot floor and spare wheel cover were designed for the S-type and 420 models. The spare wheel and tool kit are revealed here, along with the new style jack that was also accommodated below the boot instead of clipped to the rear bulkhead as with the other models.

circular knob in the centre top of the door card that did the job. This was another of those occasional throw-backs to Jaguar's earlier days, as the same knob had been used on 1950s models like the Mark VII saloon!

The rear doors incorporated a combined armrest and pocket running virtually the full width of the door. This still incorporated the same style of chromed ashtray as was used in the other models.

Headlining

Headlining was of the same type and style as fitted to the Mk 2 initially, but in September 1966 this changed to match the later Daimlers with a solid fixing to the roof and accompanying roll finish to the sides.

Boot

The boot interior was exactly the same for S-type, 420 and Sovereign models. As well as being much larger and more practical than that of the Mk 1, Mk 2 and Daimler derivatives, it was a little plusher in finish.

Although it still retained a black Hardura shaped matting which was clipped to the boot floor in the usual way, separate pieces of Hardura were glued to the body floor where it met the sides and also on the raised rear floor area over the axle; they also continued up the vertical section of the rear bulkhead. The board side panels to the inner wings were coloured black and attached in the same way as the others, and the interior of the boot lid now had Hardura panelling glued in the spaces within the support frame.

The boot lid was now secured closed by two locks, one either side. These were controlled by a single catch from the outside, and were connected to each latch by rods.

The rear inner wings now not only incorporated the two

fuel pumps but also the fuel tanks. The space beneath the boot floor was still left for the spare wheel, which was mounted and placed very much as on the Mk 2. Again, it provided a home for the fitted tool kit. However, the jack and wheelbrace were now accommodated in a black Hardura bag left loose in the boot area.

While the boot lid interior of Mk 1, Mk 2 and Daimler V8 models was left plain in body paint finish, for the S-type 420 and Sovereign models, the inner panel area between the metal bracing was covered in black Hardura matting that was glued to the body.

The boot interior area was the same for S-type, 420 and Sovereign models, still retaining Hardura (black) matting but with extra Hardura finishing trim at either side to cover the longitudinal member of the 'chassis'. The boarding covering the inner wing areas was now black.

BODY AND TRIM

This early 2.4 litre (Mk 1) owned by Michael Bing represents the very first post-war small chassisless saloon produced by Jaguar.

The original monocoque (chassisless) construction of the 2.4-litre was somewhat over-engineered as it was new territory for Jaguar at the time. Nevertheless it proved highly successful, as the basic structure remained unchanged throughout the production of all the models covered in this publication.

The shell was made up entirely of steel by the Pressed Steel Company. Two perimeter channel sections ran from the very front of the body to the rear wheel arch area, with spring anchorage on each side, and were welded to the ribbed floor to form box sections. A number of transverse members joined the main structure front to rear. The whole structure was tied together by the bulkhead at the front and the seat pan at the rear. There were two further box sections that ran diagonally up each side of the engine bay, adding further strength to the structure.

Outer sills welded to the main structure formed part of the overall structure of the car, and were common to all models. All the inner and outer body panels were also welded to the main structure, the only bolt-on panels being the door assemblies, the boot, the bonnet and the rear wheel spats.

For the Mk 2, significant changes were made to both the outer structure and the panelling. In the main unitary construction the roof line was altered, flattened out and widened to accommodate the new window areas. Jaguar offered two bodyshells for these cars, one without and one with a metal sunroof, the latter now being very rare.

For the S-type and 420 an almost complete re-design of the monocoque was required, along with significant changes to some outer panelling. To start with, the bodyshell was longer by 7 inches. The changes included flattening out the roof panel and extending it slightly to accommodate a larger, slightly deeper and more steeply raked rear screen. The rear seat pan and back area was totally re-designed to accommodate the independent rear suspension cage, as the Mk 2 shell in this area was never intended to take that weight or any associated stress. 'Middle' sills were also fitted to these models to increase the torsional stiffness of the whole body.

The changes at the front for the S-type did not necessitate any internal panel amendments and externally even used the

Significant changes were made to the outer structure and panels for the Mk2. The roof line was altered and glass area increased.

same bonnet pressing as the Mk 2. However, other front panels were different.

There was another entirely different frontal treatment for the 420 and Sovereign models. This necessitated a new bonnet pressing, and these models also had different inner wings with much more under bonnet space. The extra space helped to accommodate the power steering pump on the left, and the larger carburettors on the right.

A radiator grille top closing panel, visible with the bonnet open, was made up from steel and welded in place across the top of both wings on all models. This contained the release mechanism for the bonnet lock and was stamped with the chassis number of that particular vehicle.

The boxed rear sections used for the leaf spring mountings on the Mk 2 shell were continued rearward over the wheel arches and under the boot floor. The floor at the rear was double-skinned and welded to these box sections for extra strength. With a deeply ribbed floor for further strength, the spare wheel well was more centrally positioned. All these changes improved the boot capacity from 12 cu ft in the Mk 1 and Mk 2 to 19 cu ft in the S-type, 420 and Sovereign models.

Finally, the rear tonneau area at the base of the rear screen and the side body areas between the boot lid and rear wings were also re-designed to fit.

All changes to the bodyshells affected both Jaguar and Daimler models equally. Lead loading, never plastic filler,

was used for all seams and for filling to smooth out lines where necessary.

The completed underside areas of the shell (including the engine bay and bonnet interior) were sprayed with a form of anti-corrosion covering known as Flintcote, leaving a mottled effect finish. The bodies were initially sprayed throughout with single-pack ICI acrylic paint (although Jaguar were well known for changing suppliers to keep costs down!)

An almost complete re-design of the monocoque was required to achieve the longer tail of the S-type, 420 and Sovereign.

99

Before the middle of 1957, the 2.4 litre had a narrow cast radiator grille with wide vertical slats and unique 'litre' badge mounting at the top. The bumper bar design remained the same throughout production of all Mk 1s, Mk 2s and Daimler V8s although the positioning of the over-riders altered with the Mk 2s and Daimlers. The two thin chromed Mazak 'spears' above the headlamps were also carried over unchanged to all Mk 2, 240, 340 and Daimler models.

Frontal area and wings

The frontal panel area of the Mk 1, Mk 2 and Daimler V8 models is very similar, with slight differences to the valance (behind the front bumper, painted to body colour) and the wings themselves. The early 2.4-litre models with the narrow cast grille had unique wings. The outer wings were welded and lead-loaded either side of the grille, onto the edge of the scuttle, and onto the front of the sills. They were also spot welded around the grille aperture, onto the underneath support panels (known as 'crow's feet'), and to the A-post panels. The tops of the outer wings were spot-welded to the inners at the top, then covered with a capping strip which continued across the front behind the grille.

The inner wings were amended from model to model to suit fixtures and fittings such as oil bath air cleaners, although the basic structure was the same throughout. The wings were joined at the front base by welding to a U-shaped cross-member, and to the 'crow's feet' (one per side), strengthened horizontal quarter panels painted in the body colour. Separate closing panels, called "baffle splash panels", were fitted behind the front wheel areas; they were welded in place and

finished in body colour. These panels had a rubber seal on the outer edge in an attempt to prevent water ingress.

The bonnet pressing remained the same on all the Mk 1, Mk 2, Daimler V8 and S-type models, a single pressing with a longitudinal support bar on the inside through which the holes were drilled to accept the captive nuts for the central chromed strip. Similar holes were provided at either side of the bonnet running the full length, for other chrome strips (see later).

The bonnet pressing for the 420 and Sovereign was similarly braced, although it was different with a flatter face. It did not have any holes drilled for the side chrome strips as none were fitted to these models.

All bonnets were finished, like the rest of the underside, with anti-corrosive treatment and painted to body colour.

At the rear of the bonnet, welded to the bulkhead, was the scuttle panel that included the scuttle ventilator. It was part of the full monocoque and the front wings were welded to it at the top. The welds here were lead loaded for smoothness and drilled to accept the riveted clips for a chrome finisher that ran horizontally with the other trims (see below).

In this front view of a Mk 2, note the slightly revised position of the over-riders to accommodate the new fog lamp arrangement, and another new radiator grille, now with a separate thick vertical chromed bar incorporating the engine size badge.

This front view of a standard equipment 240 shows the dummy horn grilles that replaced the fog lamps.

The bonnets were all rear hinged by two metal hinges with tensioned springs. Hinges and springs were finished in body colour, and were held in place to the bonnet underframe and to the bulkhead by four threaded bolts per side. At the front, the bonnet was held down by a conventional spring-loaded catch, with spring and latch all in body colour, both secured to the bonnet and body by nuts and bolts. The catch was operated by a cable running down the right side of the inner wing and passing through the bulkhead to a black pull handle knob under the dashboard. A further safety catch kept the bonnet down in case the latch released when the car was being driven. Also in body colour, this was released from a 'notch' countersunk hole in the radiator grille top panel by a push up lever.

The front wings on Mk 1s came in just two types. Those for the original cast radiator grille 2.4 litres had the area around the grille shaped accordingly. With the introduction of the 3.4 litre model and the new wider grille, new front wings were produced.

The front wings for the Mk 2 (and Daimler V8) were identical from the mid-wheelarch area back, but the frontal section was totally re-designed to accommodate the new lighting

The front of the S-type model shows the clear differences between it and the Mk 2 range. There was yet another new radiator grille with a more prominent surround, although it still incorporated the same engine size badge as other models.

The 420 adopted the more contemporary approach to Jaguar saloon styling with the four-headlamp treatment and a slight forward lean for the radiator grille. For the Daimler model, another fluted grille was adopted with a gold 'D' emblem set within a plastic badge on top. The Art Deco styled D mascot was carried over from the V8 models as well as the triangular section centre bonnet chrome.

arrangements. To accommodate the new side lights, a separate pod-like pressing was welded into the top of the wings.

Front wings for the S-type were again totally new pressings but as with the Mk 2, rear sections were unchanged in style and design. The front wing changes included the peaked area above the headlamp surrounds, more prominent and slightly peaked surrounds for the fog lamps, and similar treatment for the wrap-around units that combined side lights and indicators.

With the introduction of the slimmer bumper bars for the S-type and then the 240, 340 and Daimler V8-250, a revised valance was used.

That brings us to the 420 and Sovereign, which needed a total re-design at the front of the car with new wings, bonnet and even inner wings. The wings were now widened to accommodate the four-headlight treatment with peaked tops and areas below to accommodate the wrap-around side-and-indicator light units from the S-type. There were drilled holes for the new rectangular chromed mock horn grilles, which were held in place by integral pins pushed into small nylon sockets.

The bonnet pressing was the same for all Mk 1, Mk 2, 240, 340, Daimler V8 and S-type models. The underside was finished with a sound deadening body Schutz, and the Daimler V8s and S-type models also had Hardura sound deadening material glued in place.

Rear area and wings

Rear wings were made up from a single pressing and welded to the car via the boot surround and tonneau panel, inner wheel arch, rear bulkhead, D-post and rear valance. The same design followed through from Mk 1 to all Mk 2 and V8 models with only slight changes for such things as access holes. On the left-hand side, a separate bolt-on fuel filler flap led to the fuel filler pipe finished in black that terminated in a bayonet-fit fuel filler (see later).

An entirely new rear under-bumper bar valance was needed for Mk 2s, with recessed areas for the exit of the

The Jaguar 420 featured a winged Jaguar badge set into the top of the grille and a smaller version of the leaper mascot in the centre of the bodywork. The bonnet now had a different pressing to all earlier cars and was shorter.

The thinner bumpers of the later cars necessitated a deeper rear body valance. The rear bumper now extended all the way forward to meet the rear wheel spats but the rubber seal between the bumper bar and bodywork remained the same length.

exhaust tailpipes on the left, as there was no such provision on the Mk 1 models. With the launch of the Daimler V8s, another new valance was needed without the recesses, as the exhaust tail-pipes exited one each side at a slightly lower level. Another new and deeper valance was needed for both the V8-250 and the 240 and 340 models because of the later slim-line bumpers. There were two versions, one with the recess for the Jaguar twin-pipe exhausts, and another without for the V8's single pipe per side.

The rear bodywork of the S-type, 420 and Sovereign was a re-design and was exactly the same for both models,

following the style of the Mark X and 420G although it was not the same as on the larger cars. The lengthening of the unitary construction had meant the pressing of new longer rear wings, braced on the inside, which carried the two saddle fuel tanks. Separate fuel fillers were fitted to each wing, now hinged from the top rather than the side as on the Mk 2 and other models.

The boot lid, originally designed for the 2.4-litre model, remained unchanged for all Mk 1, Mk 2 and Daimler V8 models except for different drillings to accept badging and trim. It was hinged from the rear, with two counter-balanced hinges

The design of the fuel filler in the rear wing, seen here on a Mk 1, remained the same through all the models with this bodywork. However the original knurled round filler cap shown here was later changed (see below).

This later type of fuel filler cap was fitted to all models from Mk 2 onwards.

With twin fuel tanks fitted to the S-type and 420 models, a different type of lid, hinged at the top, was fitted.

(one per side) bolted to the car's tonneau panel and painted in body colour. The lid had a quite simple curved design and incorporated strengthening sections on the underside which was devoid of any trim or sound deadening finish; instead the whole underside facing was finished in body colour. The counter-balancing mechanism ran horizontally under the tonneau panel, also painted in the body colour.

For the S-type, 420 and Sovereign models, the new, larger and more angled boot lid was of a similar structure and had similar hinges but it also had three black Hardura sound deadening panels glued between the bracings. The boot light was quite innovative, being operated by a mercury tilt switch.

Another new style of deeper rear valance was necessary for the S-type, 420 and Sovereign models. It had no recesses for the twin tail pipes, which were now separate underneath the valance and were themselves secured by rubber brackets to the boot floor.

Doors

All doors were also made of steel with a braced inner framework and bracketry to accommodate the lock and winder mechanisms and the window channels. All doors had a pressed mid-point horizontal line from the front door forward edge through to the rear door rear edge, and this was drilled to accommodate the rivets and clips for chromed trims. Cast aluminium hinges attached the doors to the A and C posts. Each hinge was secured into the body by four cross-headed countersunk set-screws, and both hinges and screws were painted in body colour. All hinges incorporated a door-check mechanism to retain doors open at an angle of about 45 degrees when required.

With the full steel door design of the Mk 1s, finisher chrome trims were fitted to all window surrounds and all doors had opening quarter-lights.

The door rubber seal arrangement was similar throughout production of all these cars. Separate rubbers were fitted to the A post section by means of a channel which was riveted in separately.

The door structure for the Mk 1s was unique in that it incorporated the complete window surrounds, somewhat over-engineered for their time. With the introduction of the Mk 2 range, a new frameless pressing was produced by removing the top section forming the window frames. From then on, these would be separate bolt-on structures, made from chrome-plated brass. On early Mk 2s they had no strengthening gussets; the later cars had small ones, and there were much stronger ones on the S-type, 420 and Sovereign models. The outer door skin was exactly the same from the waist level down for all post-Mk 1 models. These doors then

Very early 2.4 litre models had the door lock mechanism painted to body colour, but it was chrome plated on all later cars.

Only the early 2.4 litre Mk 1s featured these full spats over the rear wheels, which were abandoned with the introduction of the 3.4 litre model.

continued to be used on all the cars covered in this book right up to the 420 and Sovereign, even though the rear wings had been changed.

Door locks were all chromed and left without paint, although some very early 2.4-litre cars had them painted body colour. The locks were produced by Wilmot Breedon to a standard design.

The outer door handles will be covered below in the Body Trims section.

Rear Wheel Spats

The tapering shape of the rear of the car and its narrow rear track meant that the original 2.4-litre cars had full depth rear spats as part of the bodywork. Jaguar had adopted this principle on other steel-wheeled cars like the XK sportscars and Mark VII saloons. Made from steel with internal bracing, the spats were sculpted to fit the wheel arch and follow the lines of the main bodywork and sill profile. They were secured by a pin at the base that slotted into a hole in a bracket welded to the inner face of the rear wing/wheelarch area; by a rectangular lip welded onto the inside upper face of the spat that clipped around the leading edge of the wheelarch; and by two Dzus fasteners through the protruding lip of the spats and into the D-post facing, only visible and accessible with the rear door open. Everything was painted to body colour.

With the introduction of the 3.4-litre models, a cut-away spat was designed and standardised on the larger-engined cars. It was fitted in exactly the same way as the full spat, and the two types were interchangeable. Cut-away spats also had to be used when wire wheels were specified for a car. These spats had a lip to their arch section, following the style of those on the front wings.

Full-depth spats were never fitted to 3.4-litre Mk 1s, or to

any Mk 2s or other derivatives. The shaping of the spats was subtly different between the Mk 1 and Mk 2 models, those on the earlier cars being around ⅛-inch deeper. Spats were abandoned during the design of the S-type, 420 and Sovereign models.

Bumpers and over-riders

All the bumper bars were of metal manufacture, chrome plated with the reverse sides painted in silver. The front bumper bar designed for the Mk 1 was used unchanged for all Mk 2 and V8 models up to the introduction of the slim-line bumpers in 1967. However, Mk 1 bumpers have their over-riders mounted further inboard, so drill holes are different.

The rear bumper bars of the Mk 1 cars are not the same as those on later models, and are very slightly narrower. When production changed from Mk 1 to Mk 2, the curvature

Bodywork for the 3.4 litre models was unaltered from the 2.4 litre models except for the radiator grille changes mentioned earlier. The cutaway rear wheel spats look the same on all the similarly bodied models featured in this publication. However, the Mk 1 type are slightly deeper at the top than those fitted to the Mk 2s and later cars. The change may have been brought about by different production methods as the cars became more popular.

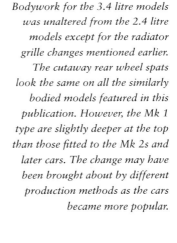

The rear bumper bar of the Mk 1s had a slightly different curvature to that fitted to the later Mk 2 models, although the style and fitment were the same. All Mk 1s, Mk 2s, 240s, 340s and Daimler V8s had a rubber seal between the bumper and the rear bodywork, with chrome finishers at each end.

With the introduction of the 240 and 340 models, an S-type styled thinner bumper bar design came in, together with revised over-rider treatment. The fog lamps were no longer a standard fit, but a special extra cost option.

For the 3.4 litre and later 2.4 litre Mk 1s, a wider radiator grille was fitted with narrower slats to aid engine cooling. This also necessitated slight changes to the wing structures. This late type of grille incorporated a special panel to accommodate the 'litre' engine size badge. Note that the car shown was built for an overseas market where Jaguar's famous leaper mascot was not allowed, and so has a longer centre bonnet chrome strip.

around the side to meet the rear wings was fractionally altered outwards. Over-rider positions are same on all models, but for the Mk 2 and Daimler holes are also drilled in the centre face to accommodate the appropriate 'disc brake' or 'D' badging in relief.

Front over-riders are not handed and are exactly the same for all these models. The rear ones are handed to allow for the curvature of the bumpers. Finished in the same way as the bumper bars, they contain an internal welded bracket drilled and tapped to take long silver bolts to secure them to the bumper bars. They have a shaped black rubber gasket, grooved to fit over the edge that faces the bumper.

The front bumper was also drilled to accept a painted black

mounting plate for the front registration plate, bolted with black nuts and bolts through the bumper itself.

All bumper bars were attached to the cars via chromed ball nuts and bolts to black painted brackets that connected directly to the chassis legs on the inner mountings, and the end of the cross member for the outer mountings. The rear bumper had a black rubber finisher seal running along the whole of its top length, and this seal was grooved to grip the bumper edge. Chromed finials at each end secured the seal to the bumper.

The slim-line front bumper bar first seen on the S-type followed the general shaping of the earlier style even down to the dipped section that fitted around the bottom of the radiator grille. The same bar was also fitted to the 240, 340 and Daimler V8-250 models without change. The slim-line bumpers for the 420 and Sovereign models were different in shape to match the widened frontal area but also slightly deeper front to rear, and did not have the central dipped area. However, they did have a cut-away section to meet the differently styled, much wider grille as it extends forward at its base.

Over-riders for these slim-line front bumpers are a bit of a mix-and-match. Those for the 240, 340 and V8 are the same. For the S-type however, the forward face slopes slightly back. For the 420 and Sovereign they are upright (as on the 240) but are deeper to accommodate the different profile of the bumper bar.

At the rear, the slim-line bumper for the 240, 340 and V8-250 was unique to these models, taking the same profile around the back of the car's bodywork and retaining the sealing strip. The centrally mounted badges were deleted as they would no longer fit the thinner bumper. The rear bumper for the S-type, 420 and Sovereign models was different, continuing further around the side along the rear wings. It followed the slim-line style and was reminiscent of the bumpers on the larger Mark X and 420G saloons, but was not the same. This bumper had to incorporate a different style of mounting at the sides with rubber bushing through the rear wings. There was no separate rubber seal fitted to the top of these bumpers.

Rear over-riders on all the slim-line bumper cars had a new style and are all the same and therefore interchangeable – but not between front and rear. All had a backwards-sloping front face like the S-type front over-riders, and the rear ones were again angled.

Radiator grilles

There were seven different types of radiator grille fitted to these models, all metal and chrome plated. All were bolted to the front wing areas by means of nuts on captive threaded studs brazed into the inner face of the grille surrounds.

For the original 2.4 litre car up to 1957, the narrow oval cast one-piece style was used with eight broad vertical ribs and an inset plastic enamelled badge (see below). An integral part of the casting was a central finisher leading up to the edge

The most notable change in the Mk 2 styling to accommodate a Daimler model was yet another new radiator grille that used the traditional Daimler fluting. The overall style at the front of the car suited this type of grille. As there was only one engine fitted to this model, there was no engine size badge. The Art Deco styled 'D' mascot stood atop the bonnet in place of the Jaguar leaper.

of the bonnet, to meet the bonnet central strip.

For the 3.4 litre Mk 1 and from 1957 the 2.4 litre model as well, a wider grille was fitted with a brass outer section with 16 slimmer, silver-soldered, vertical vanes made of brass. A separate casting formed the badge mounting at the top centre that also continued back to meet the bonnet strip.

For all Mk 2 and the 240 and 340 models, the grille took the same style and shape as the later Mk 1s but had only 12

Radiator grille badges

The list below applied to all Mk 1s, Mk 2s, 240s, 340s and S-types. There was no grille badging on the Daimler V8s.

2.4 litre engines	Legend '2.4 litre'	Gold outer, maroon inner
3.4 litre engines	Legend '3.4 litre'	Red outer, maroon inner
3.8 litre engines	Legend '3.8 litre'	Maroon outer, silver inner

For the Jaguar 420, a chromed wings emblem was fitted. Ribbed horizontally in four sections, it incorporated a black central plastic insert with the Jaguar name in silver. This was the same badge used on the Mark X and 420G models.
For the Daimler Sovereign, a circular moulded plastic badge was inset into the grille surround top, with a black background and a script 'D' in gold.

vertical ribs with a separate, bolt-on prominent central rib incorporating the badging and again continuing back to meet the bonnet strip.

For the Daimler V8 models another new grille was used. Taking the same style and size to fit the existing Mk 2 wings, this one had a heavier chromed surround with 22 vertical ribs in the opening and a prominent central rib that formed part of the surround casting. This pressing was much larger and pronounced, incorporated the traditional Daimler fluting and continued back to meet the bonnet edge without any badging.

For the S-type there was yet another new grille design, taking the general form of that for the Mk 2. It had 14 vertical ribs, and a more substantial chromed surround that stood proud of the ribs. The central rib was similar but not the same in shape as that fitted to the Mk 2.

For the 420 and related Sovereign there were two grilles, one for the Jaguar and the other for the Daimler. Both took their styling cues from the grille fitted to the 420G, and were more angular in shape than other types, shorter in depth and sloped forwards to match the line of the front panels. The Jaguar's chromed surround had a peak at the top and incorporated drillings for the winged badge (see below). It finished in a chromed spear to meet up with the bonnet chromed strip. Two panels of 16 vertical ribbed panels, with each rib riveted to a frame, were bolted to the inside of the grille, with a central thicker rib forming part of the surround casting.

The only difference for the Daimler Sovereign grille was a different surround with traditional fluting, a more substantial size to the framework, and Daimler badging.

Radiator badging also varied. Badging for the Mk 1, Mk 2, 240 and 340 and the S-type took the form of a circle moulded from plastic and painted from the inside with different legends as appropriate, including the Jaguar name at the top and the engine size at the bottom. The design remained the same but colours differed according to engine size. A centrally engraved growler head was painted gold with an engine-turned radiated fan design as background, surrounded by a gold line. There was an outer section of colour with the legends in gold and a further outer line in gold.

Mascots

Three styles of bonnet mascot were fitted to these cars. All Jaguars had a chromed Mazak leaper that took the traditional form as used on other models. However, although the larger mascot fitted to the Mk 1, Mk 2, 240, 340 and S-type models was the same as many other leaper castings, it had a different base to match the chrome strip on the bonnet, with a notch in the rear to latch onto the strip. The mascots were bolted through to the bonnet via two threaded studs and bolts.

For the 420 a much smaller leaper was fitted, the same as that used on the Mark X and 420G, but again with a different mounting to suit the bonnet strip. This time there was no interconnecting notch in the design. The leaper in this

The large chromed Mazak leaping mascot was a standard fit on UK Mk 1s, Mk 2s, 240s, 340s and S-type models – but only on some cars destined for overseas markets. It was fitted between chromed strips on the bonnet and although of the same size as many used on other Jaguar models, its base mounting was different.

All Mk 1s had waistline chrome trims following the style and design of those used on the bonnet sides. Sized to allow space for the door handles, these trims followed the styling line of the car down to the rear bumper, and that style was repeated on the Mk 2s, 240s, 340s and Daimler V8s.

instance was not mounted onto the bonnet itself but on the scuttle panel between the grille and bonnet.

The Daimler models were treated differently, with a stylised 'D' forming a chromed Mazak mascot with a triangular chromed base to match the different style of bonnet trim used on all of the Daimler cars (see below). This Daimler emblem was fitted to the bonnet of the V8 models in the same way as the leaper on Jaguars, and for the Sovereign it was mounted on the scuttle panel between grille and bonnet.

Body Trims

All these models were substantially adorned with chrome trim, most of which was pressed brass and hollow inside, held in place with rivets, clips and small bolts through the bodywork.

Bonnet chromes were the same half moon design for all models except Daimlers, which used a triangular section trim, all attached to the bonnet by their clips. For all models except the 420 and Sovereign these bonnet strips were accompanied by chrome trims with the same section around the left and right hand side edges of the bonnet, secured in the same way.

Swage line chromes were again of the same section for ALL models. On later cars they were attached by press stud clips, themselves riveted into the car's bodywork. The swage line chromes comprised a finisher to the scuttle area (between the bonnet and door chromes), single-piece trims for each door and, for the Mk 1, Mk 2, 240, 340 and V8s, another finisher trim leading down from the D-post to meet the rear bumper. On the S-type, 420 and Sovereign models a spear finisher was fitted to the scuttle sides, and shorter spears on the rear wings.

Apart from the Mk 1s, all models featured the by then traditional brass window frames, chromium plated and incorporating quarter lights front and rear. Very early Mk 2 frames were prone to flexing, and so (as mentioned earlier) for all later models strengtheners were brazed to the lower section of the frames before chrome plating. These window surrounds were similar but not the same for all post-Mk 1 models, and on the S-types, 420s and Sovereigns they were stronger.

Roof rain guttering was an integral part of the bodywork on all models, but for all post-Mk 1 models chromed finishers

The Mk 1 Jaguars were the only ones with these Wilmot Breeden door handles. Both driver's and front passenger door had external key locks.

The Mk 2 had separate window frames made of chromed brass. The different style also incorporated quarter lights in all doors and the new shape of the frames necessitated alterations to the chrome rain gutters and even the roof line.

were a push-fit onto the bodywork. They were made up of two sections each side, mated in the centre with a chromed clip to hide the join.

Exterior door furniture was the same for all cars, except for the Mk 1s. The Mk 1s used a contemporary style of push-button door handle, also fitted to other cars such as Rover P4s. All door furniture was made of Mazak and chromed, but only the driver's door handle incorporated a Wilmot Breedon key lock. All handles were secured to the car via their threaded studs and nuts (two per lock).

For the Mk 2, 240 and 340, Daimler V8s, S-types, 420s and Sovereigns, a more sculpted design of door handle was fitted,

the same as that used on Jaguar's other contemporary saloons like the Mark X and 420G.

Brightwork trim at the rear had a similar style for all models even though bodywork shaping was different. All cars had a chromed Mazak number plate nacelle with illumination and reversing light. Starting with the Mk 1, Mk 2, 240 and 340, this incorporated a Lucas frosted reversing light lens embossed with the word 'Jaguar'. Underneath, within the same light unit, was the number plate illumination bulb of 21watt. The whole unit was bolted to the boot lid via a shaped black gloss rubber gasket and threaded studs and bolts. A single chromed half-moon section finisher, clipped to the

The Mk 2s had a new design of door handle that was retained for all other models covered in this book. Both front doors featured external key locks.

Although the front quarter lights on all models followed normal practice in style and operation, the rear door quarter-lights on Mk 2s and all subsequent models featured in this publication had a more sophisticated method of operation, a feature first seen on Jaguars back in the late 1940s and taken from contemporary Bentleys.

There was no boot badging on the 2.4 litre Mk 1, but with the introduction of the 3.4 litre model, a scripted Jaguar badge appeared along with one indicating the engine size. Where automatic transmission was fitted, an additional badge indicated the fact.

Chrome waist trim followed the same practice as the Mk 2, but for the S-type and 420 models with their different rear bodywork, a spear finished off the trim at this point.

boot lid, led vertically down from the nacelle and across the bottom to form a number plate surround. The same applied to the Daimler V8s except that they had traditional fluting to the chromed top of the nacelle and the rear light lens carried the Daimler name.

The S-type, 420 and Sovereign models had a different style of nacelle, of a flatter design with twin reversing light units, one either side of the central badge section which had an embossed 'Jaguar' name in the casting. As well as providing number plate illumination from underneath, it was cut away

to accommodate the boot release mechanism and key lock. For the Daimler Sovereign, the Jaguar name in the casting was covered by a black plastic badge with a gold Daimler identification, and the casting was drilled to accept a single secured nut and bolt.

Other badging

Badging on the boot varied. All badges were attached by studs built into the casting, secured to the car via small rubber sleeves, into spire clips.

Engine size badging appeared on all Mk 1 models, here shown in 2.4 litre form on the original cast radiator grille and in 3.4 litre form on the later wider grille with its separate chromed holder. The same style of engine size badging followed through on all Mk 2, 240 and 340 models.

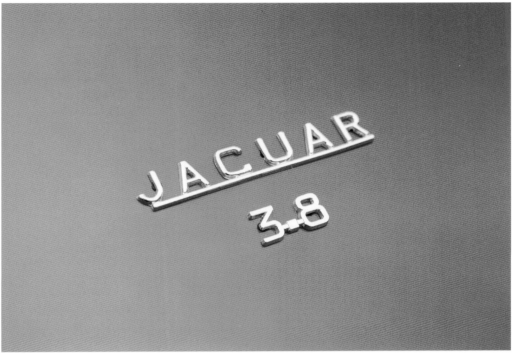

With the introduction of all round disc brakes as standard on all Mk 2 models, a warning badge was fitted to the centre of the rear bumper bar, enamelled in red. [Following drivers needed to be aware of how quickly these cars could stop!]

The original 2.4 litre Mk 1 did not have any boot badging at all. From late 1957, the Jaguar name was added in a scripted form (the same badging as used on other Jaguar models of the period), on both 2.4 and 3.4 litre models. Only the 3.4 litre had a boot badge identifying the engine size (also scripted) and where automatic transmission was specified, an 'automatic' scripted badge was also used.

With the introduction of the Mk 2 the style of badging changed to one that became the norm for all subsequent Jaguar models (including all those featured here), up to the introduction of the XJ Series 2 models in the 1970s. All the cars featured here from then featured a Jaguar name in capitals and underlined, with similar treatment for the other accompanying badges. As before, 2.4 litre engined cars did not have an engine size badge and the 3.4, 3.8 and 4.2 litre engined cars all featured badging in the new style. Automatic transmission models also had new badging with underlining to match the new style Jaguar font.

Mk 2s also displayed a discreet 'Mk 2' badge at the bottom right-hand side of the boot lid. The later 240 and 340

Badging came in for revision with the introduction of the Mk 2 and remained unaltered throughout the production of these Jaguar models. A much cleaner design was adopted with the underlined Jaguar name which now appeared on all these cars – even the 2.4 litre engine model. The engine size badge, however, appeared on all Jaguar Mk 2 models except the 2.4 litre car.

The equivalent engine size badge for the 3.8 litre models is shown here mounted on the thick central bar of the Mk 2 radiator grille.

The Mk 2 models were always known as this (whereas the Mk 1 cars only got that name afterwards, and then never officially). The boot lids on all models were therefore fitted with an appropriate badge like this.

Badging was simplified for the 240 and 340 models, with a single new style engine size badge fitted to the bottom right of the boot lid. All other badging was eliminated from both the 240 and 340 except when automatic transmission was fitted.

A new style of badge was used for the Daimler V8-250 model with no other Daimler name except for that embossed into the glass of the reversing light.

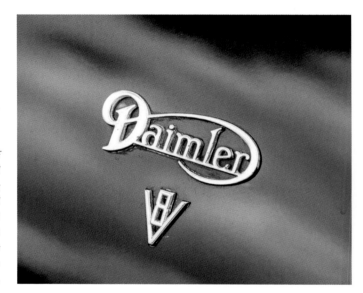

This 'D' emblem replaced the disc brake badge on the rear bumper of Daimlers. Perhaps it was felt inappropriate that Daimler drivers should want to be ostentatious enough to warn other drivers of their car's braking capabilities!

The only badging on the boot of the Daimler 2.5 litre V8 model was the script shown here along with a confirmation that this had a V8 engine fitted. As the 2.5 litre V8 cars were only fitted with automatic transmission (except to special order), there was no appropriate badging on the boot.

S-type badging followed the style of the Mk 2 but the litre engine size badge now incorporated the S letter as well.

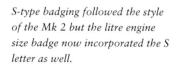

For the Daimler Sovereign model, this was the badging used on the boot lid, along with 'automatic' in the centre of the boot lid where applicable.

Front screens differed from model to model and in the case of the Mk 1s were installed from the inside of the car; most others were installed from the outside. Chrome surrounds are also subtly different between Mk 1 and Mk 2 models. All the cars here featured two chromed windscreen washer jets as shown.

models were treated differently in that they no longer carried the Jaguar name badge on the boot, nor an 'automatic' badge where applicable. Instead, they had a '240' or '340' badge at the bottom right-hand side of the boot lid.

Daimler V8s were treated differently again with a scripted 'Daimler' name in the centre of the boot lid and a 'V8' emblem below (plus 'automatic' where applicable). In the case of the V8-250, a simplified approach like that on the 240s and 340s followed with no other badging except for 'V8' and '250' at the bottom right-hand side of the boot lid.

S-types and 420s followed the same badge design and fitting as the Mk 2, except that they never carried an S-type or 420 insignia. By contrast, the Daimler Sovereign did carry the 'Daimler' and 'Sovereign' emblems in normal Jaguar font at the bottom right hand side of the boot lid, even though it did not display an engine size or even 'automatic' where applicable.

Windscreens and Wipers

Windscreens were not all the same. The Mk 1's was unique, and it was also designed to be fitted from the inside of the car! The later models were all the same, normally made from standard toughened glass, although laminated glass was obligatory in some export markets and could be specified as an extra-cost option elsewhere.

Rear screens were totally different from Mk 1 to Mk 2 (the latter incorporating the Daimler V8), the later type being much larger and deeper to provide better visibility. A differently shaped rear screen was fitted to the S-type, 420 and Sovereign models. Mk 1s were never fitted with heated elements, but this was an extra cost option on Mk 2s and originally on S-types. It became standard on later S-types and was always standard on 420s and Daimler models.

Front and rear screen rubbers were black and incorporated grooves to accommodate metal chromed surrounds. There were two sections per front screen, one outer seal and one locking strip, with chrome finishers top and bottom to hide the joins between the two trims. The Mk 1s had a one-piece rear chrome with one joining piece. To reaffirm the difference between the rubbers of the Mk 1 and other models, note that the screens were installed from the inside with the earlier cars, but from the outside on all Mk 2s and later models.

Windscreen wipers and blades (two per car) remained the same throughout production. Manufactured by Trico with rubber blades, they were made of stainless steel with accompanying stainless steel trim. They operated creating an arc (rainbow fashion) and always parked on the driver's side – LHD and RHD parking arrangements therefore differed. The wiper arms were mounted as a push fit onto splined spindles that passed through the scuttle panel to the wiper rack leading to the motor. The spindles were secured to the scuttle by a rubber gasket and chromed nuts. Rubber blades were of 11-inch length on the Mk 1 and 12 inches on all other models and within their bright surrounds were clipped to the arms in a conventional manner.

TOOLS AND HANDBOOKS

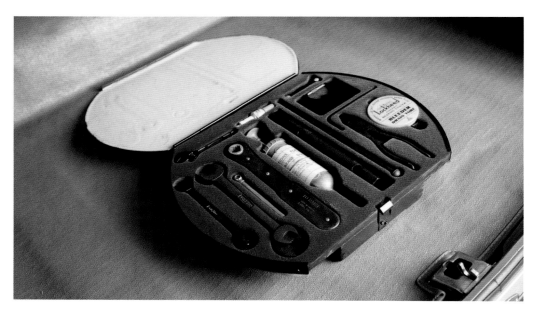

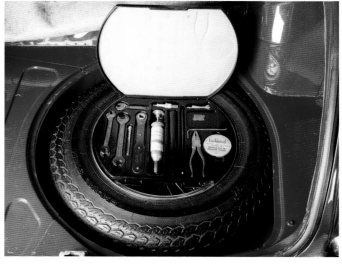

The later tool kit came in a plastic moulded box.

A comprehensive tool kit was supplied with all the cars featured in this publication. The very first 2.4 litre models had a simple black Hardura tool roll, but when large-scale production got under way, this was replaced by what you see here. It was a comprehensive range of tools that varied very little over the life of the cars, although the manufacturing material for the box altered much later and by the time of Mk 2 production, the green baize covering gave way to matt black paint! These tool kits were made to fit neatly inside the spare wheel beneath the boot floor.

Jaguar had always been well known for the extensive tool kit supplied with their cars as standard equipment, and that trend continued with the models covered in this book. The tools 'package' was initially designed for the Mk 1, but was later adapted in various forms for all the other Jaguar saloons from the period covered in this book, and was only abandoned with the introduction of the XJ6 in the late 1960s.

Tool Roll

The very first 2.4 litre models produced carried a simple tool roll of a black Hardura design with a fold-over top and pockets to accommodate the range of tools. These included a screwdriver, various spanners, a box spanner, spanner bar and pliers. This early tool roll was supplied only with a few cars (the exact number is unknown), and was perhaps issued because the new fitted tool box was not available in time for the start of production.

The car's jack and wheelbrace were always mounted separately, and in the case of Mk 1s and Mk 2s they were clipped to the underside of the rear parcel shelf with push-fit

spring steel clips. In the case of the jack, a leather strap secured the jacking point bar and handle to the main structure of the tool. For the S-type, 420 and Sovereign models, both the wheelbrace and jack were fitted to the boot floor spare wheel well, the former to the rear vertical edge (in the rear valance area) and the latter to the right-hand side. Both were secured by fabric or leather straps.

Tool Box

The fitted tool box was typical of Jaguar's attention to detail, as it was made to fit in the inner face of the spare wheel under the boot floor, where it was easily accessible when needed. It comprised a metal circular shaped box painted black with a hinged lid and spring clip fastener. Inside, the lid was fitted with grey foam material to prevent movement and vibration of the tools, and the tray itself was initially in a green flock finish on wood with cut-outs for the various tools. Variations on this type of box were fitted to all the cars featured in this book. For clarity, the contents are listed below, showing the differences between the various models.

From the mid-Sixties the flock finish of the cut-out base was

Although the boot floor covering here is not original, this picture shows the design and fitment of the jack and wheelbrace for the Mk 1 and all subsequent models up to the introduction of the S-type and 420 models.

replaced by a matt black paint. By 1966 the metal box was replaced by a cheaper moulded black plastic type with plastic hinges and two plastic clip fasteners at the front. This later type of tool box was supplied with all the subsequent models in this book, including Daimlers.

The S-type rear compartment, showing the tool kit fitted within the spare wheel and the later style jack for these models, carried inside the spare wheel well. Arrangements were the same on 420s and Sovereigns.

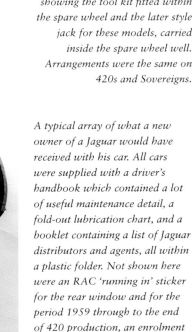

A typical array of what a new owner of a Jaguar would have received with his car. All cars were supplied with a driver's handbook which contained a lot of useful maintenance detail, a fold-out lubrication chart, and a booklet containing a list of Jaguar distributors and agents, all within a plastic folder. Not shown here were an RAC 'running in' sticker for the rear window and for the period 1959 through to the end of 420 production, an enrolment pamphlet for the Jaguar Drivers' Club. Note also here the later tool kit compared to the earlier one illustrated opposite.

TOOLS

The first list shows the standard tools supplied. All were finished in matt black unless otherwise stated and most carried the Jaguar name embossed into each tool. They were mainly manufactured by Carrington; occasionally, as a result of stock shortages or later replacements, some Carrington tools are seen in these kits that do NOT carry the Jaguar name but are otherwise identical. In Daimler toolkits it is also possible to find open-ended spanners with the "Daimler" name.

Tool	Application(s)	Part number
Small adjustable spanner	2.4, 3.4 and early Mk 2	C4651
Small adjustable spanner	Mk 2 onwards	C.23296
Pair of pliers – natural metal teeth	All	C.996
Tyre pressure gauge – chrome	All	C.11753
Screwdriver for adjustment of distributor points	All	C.5444
Feeler Gauge – natural metal	All	C.5587
Extractor, Tyre Valve – natural metal	All	C.993
Screwdriver – wooden handle	Mk 1 and early Mk 2	C.4585
Screwdriver – black plastic handle	Mk 2 onwards	C.20482
Screwdriver for battery terminals	All	C.10154
Box spanner for spark plugs and cylinder head nuts	All	C.10155
Tommy bar for box spanner	All	C.2896
Open ended spanner, 3/4in x 7/8in AF	All	C.4594
Open ended spanner, 9/16in x 7/8in AF	All	C.4595
Open Ended Spanner, 7/16in x 1/2in AF	All	C.4596
Open Ended Spanner, 11/32in x 5/8in AF	All	C.4638
Brake bleeder tube in tin, marked with Dunlop triangle	Mk 1, very early Mk 2	C.2958
Brake bleeder tube in tin, marked Dunlop	Mark 2 onwards	C.13620
Bleeder wrench	All	C.2957
Valve timing gauge	All	C.3993
Grease gun (with paper instructional leaflet)	Up to chassis numbers 908323 and 942541	C.10176
Grease gun (with paper instructional leaflet)	All later chassis numbers	C.13269
Single replacement N5 spark plug	Engines with 8:1 or 9:1 compression ratio	C.2460
Single replacement L7 spark plug	Engines with 7:1 compression ratio	C.11952
Single replacement UN12Y spark plug	Engines with 7:1, 8:1 and 9:1 compression ratios; mid-term Mk 2 on	[No number quoted
Ratchet Lever to operate Jack	All except S-type, 420 and Sovereign	C.2954

The following tools were also carried, outside the tool box.

Tool	Application(s)	Part number
Wheel brace	Not supplied on cars equipped with wire wheels from the factory (Mk 1 and early Mk 2)	C.2955
Wheel brace	Not always supplied on cars equipped with wire wheels from the factory (later Mk 2 onwards). Some cars did receive one because the flattened end could be used as a removal tool for the rear wheel spats and nave covers.	C.22401
Jack	Mk 2	C.10659
Jack	S-type, 420 and Sovereign	C.29805
Black leather or fabric strap to secure jack handle to jack	All, but rarely seen on S-type, 420 and Sovereign	C.10792

There were also several items that were supplied loose in the boot, as follows.

Tool	Application(s)	Part number
Copper and hide tipped hammer, with wooden shaft	Supplied loose on cars fitted with wire wheels from the factory (Mk 1 & early Mk 2 models)	C.992
Metallic alloy head mallet with wooden shaft	Supplied loose on cars fitted with wire wheels from the factory (Mk 2 onwards)	C.27290
Tool for removal of non-eared hub caps	Cars for Germany and Switzerland, and post-1968 models	C.14927
Nave plate removal tool	Mid-term Mk 2 onwards (sometimes also included in the tool box area but without its own cut-out space).	C.26864

Handbooks

Jaguar used the same size and format (approximately A5) of handbook and paper stock for all their cars from the mid-1950s through to the late 1960s. The content obviously changed according to model, and the colour of the card cover also changed. Variations from the list below may have applied to overseas markets where text was in a different language.

Other Paperwork

As well as the owner's handbook, new customers would have also received a range of other documents, as follows.
• Period Maintenance Voucher Book (usually black cover, landscape format)
• Large fold-out poster Maintenance Chart (usually cream paper stock with red and black content)
• Sales & Service Facilities booklet, approximately A5 size, in portrait format (usually dark blue)
• Running In sticker (usually supplied by the RAC)
• Any additional supplementary information referring to changes in specification not covered in the handbook, instructions for a radio if fitted, and from 1958 a two-colour A5 leaflet on the Jaguar Drivers' Club.

When new, this paperwork came in a plastic folder. Various types were used over the years, and to some extent the type supplied depended on what was in stock at the time. It is therefore not possible to identify by date or chassis number when one type of folder succeeded another, but a rough guide would be as follows.

1950s to early 1960s: Brown plastic with clear front, fold-over closure with brown press stud button and hot foil Jaguar wings logo in centre
Mid 1960s to early 1970s: Brown plastic with clear front, fold-over closure with heat seamed press stud and hot foil Jaguar wings logo on front panel

Later folders were fold-over types in red or blue with internal clear pockets and a hot foil Jaguar wings logo in the centre of the front cover. There is no record of when these replaced the earlier type of folder, and some owners have used them where an original earlier folder has been missing.

Examples of the handbooks for these models, produced with different coloured covers according to model. The 420 and Sovereign handbooks were printed in a landscape format whereas the others were in portrait format. Other items that might have been included in the new owner's pack would have been radio instructional leaflets, accessory leaflets or, as shown here, a wiring diagram for a rear-mounted radio speaker and after-market warranty cards.

HANDBOOKS

2.4 litre (Mk 1)	Pale Blue with Dark Blue script; portrait format
3.4 litre (Mk 1)	Black with Green script; portrait format
2.4 litre (Mk 2)	Beige with Black script; portrait format
3.4 litre (Mk 2)	Yellow with Maroon script; portrait format
3.8 litre (Mk 2)	Dark Green with Black script; portrait format
2.5 litre (Daimler V8)	Black with White Script; portrait format
3.4 litre and 3.8 litre S-type	Dark Green with White Script; portrait format
420	Turquoise with Cream script; landscape format
Sovereign (Daimler)	Mid-Green with Dark Green script; landscape format
240	Beige with Dark Blue script; portrait format
340	Yellow with Black script; portrait format

OPTIONAL EXTRAS

There were comprehensive listings of optional extras offered by the factory from time to time which could be fitted before delivery to the dealership, or by the dealer before collection by the customer. Then there were other recommended options which could be supplied and fitted by the dealer upon request. These were not always from Jaguar's own parts bin, but in some cases came from after-market suppliers. The lists below are split into categories by model, and there are notes on some items after the main lists.

MK 1

Body

Cut-away rear wheel spats for early 2.4 litre models
Exterior metal sun visor to fit above windscreen
GB emblem for boot lid, made of chromium plated brass (bolted through with threaded studs and nuts)
Lockable filler cap
Modified locks to enable all to be opened with a single key
KL radiator blind
Witter tow bar, bolted through the boot floor and emerging through the centre bumper bar area

Brakes

Conversion kit to modify drum braked cars to disc brakes

Electrical

Master battery cut-off safety switch
Double life Exide 12-volt battery
Twin windtone horns

Engine and exhaust

9:1 compression ratio 3.4 litre engine
Cut-off switch mechanism to isolate automatic choke system on 3.4 litre engines
Lead bronze engine bearings
Lightened flywheel
Twin-pipe exhaust system (2.4 litre models only)

Glass

Laminated windscreen
Rear window demister (permanently connected)

Interior fittings

Perspex internal sun visors
Vanity mirror for passenger sun visor
Gear lever extension

Numerous styles of wing mirror were available for these cars, and although Jaguar recommended certain types, in many cases it was down to the supplying dealership to supply and therefore obtain the profit from the fitment.

Sports wing mirrors were very popular in their day and they included this Sebring style where the glass was adjustable inside the casing without the casing moving.

Chromium plated grab rail to passenger side of dashboard
Pyrene fire extinguisher
Rheostat for interior dashboard lighting
White finished Bluemels steering wheel (export markets only)

Lighting
Desmo rally lamp
Le Mans 40/45-watt headlamp units

Radio and aerial
Radiomobile 200 manual tuning set
Ekco push button self-seeker set
Motorola 821 push button self-seeker set
Extension 4-inch speaker fitted to rear parcel shelf under a rectangular or oval grille; the grille could be painted black or bronze, depending on the supplier
Roof mounted chromed radio aerial (semi-retractable) with angled joint
Wing mounted chromed radio aerial, retractable
Wing mounted chromed radio aerial, fully retractable and remotely operated from winding handle and cable, normally situated under driver's side dashboard area

Seating and belts
Sports bucket seat conversion for front seat driver and passenger
Split style bench front seating (standard on automatic transmission models)
Driver's seat bracket to raise seat height adjustment
Delaney Gallay RKN front seat belts

Steering
High-ratio steering box (a standard fit on earlier cars)

Suspension
Stiffer shock absorbers
Heavy-duty anti-roll bar (¾in instead of ⅝in)

Transmission
Laycock de Normanville overdrive kit, including rear axle
Close ratio gearbox (manual transmission only)
Competition clutch
Borg Warner DG automatic transmission
Thornton Powr-Lok limited slip differential for 3.4 litre cars

Wheels and tyres
Wire wheels in silver, body colour or chrome
Set of four or five chromium-plated 15-inch rimbellishers, with clips and screw fasteners
Set of four Ace Mercury Turbo wheel discs
Goodyear Eagle tyres
Dunlop Town & Country tyres
Dunlop Weathermaster rear tyres

Lifeguard tyre tubes
Whitewall tyre finishes
Michelin X tyres (with recalibrated speedometer)
Dunlop Fort tyre tubes
Duraband tubed tyres
India Super Tyres
Dunlop Road Speed tyres

In addition, Jaguar made available three special tuning kits for the 2.4-litre models only.

Stage 1 (raising the engine output to 119bhp)
Flat type throttle spindles
25mm carburettor chokes
120mm carburettor jets
190mm air correction jets
60mm pump jets

A radio was often fitted as an accessory and various types were available along with an extendable aerial. Most aerials were vertically mounted to the rear of the front driver's side wing, but for a little extra money (because the headlining had to be adjusted), a roof mounted aerial like this looked so much better.

Electrically operated radio aerials were around during the period of production, but were rarely fitted to these cars. However, a remote wind-up aerial was a more common fit, particularly on the more expensive models like the 420. It came with a handle under the dashboard, which operated a cable to extend or retract an aerial mounted on the driver's side front wing.

Among the most popular radios fitted to Jaguars in this period were those manufactured by His Master's Voice (HMV) or, as in this case, Motorola, with five pre-select station buttons.

Although not obligatory at the time, seat belts were an option which could be fitted at the factory before delivery, or by the supplying dealership. Britax was the favoured brand.

Stage 2 (raising the engine output to 131bhp)
As for Stage 1, plus:
High lift camshafts
Twin-pipe exhaust system
Replacement valve springs
New distributor

Stage 3 (raising the engine output to 150bhp)
As for Stage 2, plus:
XK140 C-type cylinder head
Revised inlet manifolding
2 x SU 1.75inch carburettors with auxiliary starting carburettor
Revised air cleaner assembly to fit above
Stronger clutch assembly

MK 2, 240, 340 AND DAIMLER V8s
Body
Triplex Sundym tinted glass all round
Steel opening sunroof conversion kit
Standard or sports type wing mounted mirrors
Modified locks to enable all to be opened with a single key
Desmo lockable filler cap
GB emblem for boot lid, made of chromium plated brass (bolted through with threaded studs and nuts)
KL radiator blind
Witter tow bar, bolted through the boot floor emerging through the centre bumper bar area

Jaguar did have special seat belts manufactured with the leaping mascot or the Daimler emblem.

Jaguar produced a special bodyshell for those ordering a new car with a metal sliding sunroof. Very few were actually sold but a popular after-market fitment at the time was a Tudor Webasto fabric sunroof which came with a fold-out Perspex wind deflector.

Competition options (not applicable to V8s)
2 x 2-inch SU carburettors
High-ratio steering box
Lightened flywheel
Competition clutch
High-lift camshafts
Auxiliary boot-mounted fuel tank with pipework
Competition wire wheels in silver or body colour
Revised rear axles (to alter ratios)

Electrical
Master battery cut-off safety switch

Engine
9:1 compression ratio (3.4 and 3.8 litre engines only)
3.8 litre straight-port engine (for 340 model)
Cut-off switch mechanism to isolate automatic choke system (on 3.4 and 3.8 litre engines)
Kenlowe electric cooling fan

Glass
Laminated windscreen
Rear window demister (initially permanently connected, later switch-operated)

Interior
Reutter reclining front seats (early variety with chromed handles and surrounds, later without)

Reclining front seats for early Daimler V8s
Reclining front seat kits to convert solid seats (not V8s)
Leather seating (for cars not equipped as standard)
Childproof locks to rear doors
Waso steering wheel lock
Integrated steering ignition/starter switch
White covered 17-inch steering wheel
Front seat belts
Pyrene fire extinguisher

Lighting
Fogranger fog and spot lighting to cars not originally supplied
Desmo rally lamp
Radio and aerial

Radio equipment
Extensive list from HMV, Radiomobile, Motorola or Ekco, with manual or self-seeking tuning
Extension 4-inch speaker fitted to rear parcel shelf under a rectangular black or chrome surround with mesh grille; type dependent on dealer supplier
Roof mounted chromed radio aerial (semi-retractable) with angled joint
Wing mounted chromed radio aerial, retractable
Wing mounted chromed radio aerial, fully retractable and remotely operated from winding handle and cable, normally situated under driver's side dashboard area

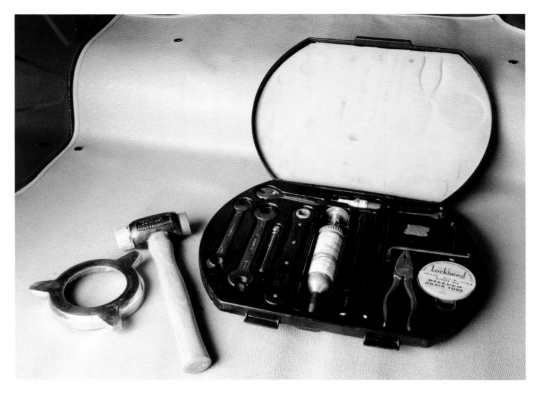

Cars specified with wire wheels were provided with a copper-headed hammer to undo and tighten the eared hubs. When changed legislation later required a new style of hub without the ears, a special adaptor had to be provided as well to give something for the hammer to 'purchase' on.

Steering
Power assisted steering for cars not so equipped

Transmission
Close ratio gearbox (manual transmission cars only)
Borg Warner automatic transmission (standard on 2.5 litre V8)
Laycock de Normanville overdrive kit, including rear axle

Wood-rim steering wheels were all the rage at the time and amongst the many options for the Mk 2 was a boss to enable an E-type steering wheel to fit. This specially produced wheel made in Birmabright polished metal [aluminium alloy] would also accept the Mk 2 horn ring and centre spokes. (Author.)

Thornton Powr-Lok limited slip differential (for 3.4 litre engine cars)

Wheels and tyres
Wire wheels in silver, body colour or chrome
Set of four or five chromium plated 15-inch rimbellishers (press fit)
Set of four Ace Mercury Turbo wheel discs
Whitewall tyre finishes
Dunlop Road Speed or SP tyres

S-TYPE
Body
Modified locks to enable all to be opened with a single key
GB emblem for boot lid, made of chromium plated brass (bolted through with threaded studs and nuts)
Standard or sports type wing mounted mirrors
KL radiator blind
Witter tow bar, bolted through the boot floor and emerging through the centre bumper bar area

Electrical
Master battery cut-off safety switch

Engine
9:1 compression ratio for 3.4 and 3.8 litre engines only
Cut-off switch mechanism to isolate automatic choke system on 3.4 and 3.8 litre engines
Kenlowe electric cooling fan

Glass
Laminated windscreen
Rear window demister (switch operated)
Triplex Sundym tinted glass all round

Interior
Childproof locks to rear doors
Waso steering wheel lock
Integrated steering, ignition and starter switch
Reclining front seats
Leather seating (for cars not equipped as standard)
Front seat belts

Lighting
Fogranger fog and spot lighting to cars not originally supplied
Radio and aerial

Radio equipment
Extensive list from HMV, Radiomobile, Motorola or Ekco, manual or self-seeking tuning
Extension 4-inch speaker fitted to rear parcel shelf under a rectangular black or chrome surround with mesh grille; type dependent on dealer supplier

Roof mounted chromed radio aerial (semi-retractable) with angled joint
Wing mounted chromed radio aerial, retractable
Wing mounted chromed radio aerial, fully retractable and remotely operated from winding handle and cable, normally situated under driver's side dashboard area

Steering
Power assisted steering for cars not so equipped

Transmission
Close ratio gearbox (manual transmission cars only)
Borg Warner automatic transmission
Laycock de Normanville Overdrive kit including rear axle
Thornton Powr-Lok limited slip differential for 3.4 litre cars

Wheels and tyres
Wire wheels in silver, body colour or chrome
Set of four or five chromium plated 15-inch rimbellishers (press fit)
Set of four Ace Mercury Turbo wheel discs
Whitewall tyre finishes
Dunlop Road Speed or SP tyres

420 and Sovereign
Body
Modified locks to enable all to be opened with a single key
GB emblem for boot lid, made of chromium plated brass (bolted through with threaded studs and nuts)
Standard or sports type wing mounted mirrors
KL radiator blind
Witter tow bar, bolted through the boot floor and emerging through the centre bumper bar area

Electrical
Master battery cut-off safety switch

Engine
Kenlowe electric cooling fan

Glass
Rear window demister, switch operated (420 only)
Triplex Sundym tinted glass all round

Interior
Air conditioning (USA market only)
Childproof locks to rear doors
Waso steering wheel lock
Integrated steering, ignition and starter switch
Rear seat belts
Leather seating (for export cars not so equipped as standard)
Front seat belts

Lighting
Fogranger fog and spot lighting to cars not originally so fitted
Radio and aerial

Radio equipment
Extensive list from HMV, Radiomobile, Motorola or Eko, with manual or self-seeking tuning
Extension 4-inch speaker fitted to rear parcel shelf under a rectangular black or chrome surround with mesh grille; type dependent on dealer supplier
Roof mounted chromed radio aerial (semi-retractable) with angled joint
Wing mounted chromed radio aerial, retractable
Wing mounted chromed radio aerial, fully retractable and

Fitted luggage was available from several specialists for all manner of cars during the 1950s and 1960s. This is one example by Auto Luggage of a set available for the Mk 2 Jaguars. (Author's archive collection.)

Where these were not standard equipment, Jaguar did supply fully reclining front seats for the cars. This example is of the more luxurious type with chromed side control and finishers. (Author's archive collection.)

Ace full wheel rimbellishers were a common accessory, eliminating the need for a separate hub cap and trim. (Author.)

remotely operated from winding handle and cable, normally situated under driver's side dashboard area

Steering
Power assisted steering (420 only)

Transmission
Borg Warner automatic transmission
Laycock de Normanville Overdrive (420 only)
Close ratio gearbox (manual transmission cars only)

Wheels and tyres
Wire wheels in silver, body colour or chrome
Set of four or five chromium plated 15-inch rimbellishers (press fit)
Set of four Ace Mercury Turbo wheel discs
Whitewall tyre finishes
Dunlop Road Speed or SP tyres

An interesting period after-market extra was this combined centre armrest and glove box, produced by the Henly's organisation that was then Jaguar's largest distributor.

Notes

Ace Mercury wheel discs
Only available for steel-wheeled cars, these replaced standard hub caps and rimbellishers as a single fit, covering the whole wheel. The discs fitted into a threaded boss inserted from behind the wheel, and were die-pressed in aluminium with a fin style around the outer surface. A separate centre section resembled the Jaguar hub cap style, complete with Jaguar emblem, and was bolted through the centre of the trim.

Wheel rimbellishers
The optional chromed ring rimbellishers were available on all models. Up to the introduction of the Mk 2, these were held to the road wheel by means of hooked clips with screws that held onto a rib on each rimbellisher. From the introduction of the Mk 2 a simple push-fit rimbellisher was used, with its own sprung surround.

Seat Belts
Seat belt anchorage points were only added to the Mk 2 bodyshell from January 1962 and these were for the front seats. They were needed to meet legislation in some overseas markets, although seat belts did not become compulsory in the UK until 1st January 1965. The approved manufacturer was Kangol, and the belts were of the three-point type with mountings on the B/C post and in the floor between the front seats. Chromed buckles were fitted, with chrome miniature leaper mascots or a Daimler 'D', and webbing was grey.

Steering Wheels
As mentioned elsewhere, three distinct types of steering wheel were fitted as standard. These were the Bluemels four-spoke traditional type for the Mk 1, and the two types of two-spoke wheel with half horn ring fitted to all other models. However, Jaguar also offered a white steering wheel for certain export markets and in addition made the E-type three-spoke wood rimmed wheel available for the Mk 2s. Extra to this, the outside supplier of Derrington produced a very attractive wood rimmed alloy wheel onto which the standard Jaguar horn ring and surround could be fitted.

Air Conditioning
Air conditioning was only ever available from the factory for the 420 and Sovereign models. It was primarily for the North American market but several right-hand-drive cars were also built with air conditioning. The system included a Sanden compressor mounted in the engine bay, belt driven off the engine. Appropriate pipework ran throughout the car, and there was an auxiliary control panel on the dashboard. Extractor ducts were usually in the rear window area, but in some cases were also fitted to the front compartment. The main part of the system, consisting of drier, evaporator, fans and wiring was mounted in the boot along the shelf area above the rear axle.

PAINT AND COLOUR SCHEMES

This section is a guide to the standard colour schemes available on these models throughout their production period. The following general notes however apply.

• Colours quoted covered all markets, though some were not available in them all.
• In some cases, over the years, totally different colours were given the same names. This can be confusing now.
• It was Jaguar practice to paint cars to specific order when requested, using colours from other Jaguar models or periods, or indeed an individual paint not normally associated with the brand. Also it was not unknown to see some cars in two-tone colour schemes; although not produced in-house at Jaguar, these were catered for at dealerships. It is not possible to cover these alternatives here.
• Although standard interior colour schemes applied to specific exterior paint finishes, it was also not unusual for purchasers to request alternatives which also cannot be covered here.
• Cars that were built up abroad from CKD (Completely Knocked Down) kits were in some cases painted in the country of assembly. These 'local' colour schemes are also not covered here. The same scenario applied to interior finishes, particularly where locally made plastic or vinyl trim and headlinings were fitted.
• None of the cars featured here were ever fitted as standard with contrast colour interior trim piping, but again this may have been specified at the time of customer ordering.

The lists that follow show the range of exterior paint and interior finishes recorded by Jaguar Cars.

2.4 and 3.4 litre Mk 1 Colour Schemes

Exterior	Interior
Arbor Green (1956 only)	Suede Green or Tan
Battleship Grey (to 1957)	Biscuit, Grey or Red
Birch Grey (to 1957)	Dark Blue, Light Blue, Grey or Red
Black	Biscuit, Grey, Red or Tan
British Racing Green	Suede Green or Tan
Carmen Red (*)	Red
Carmine Red (from mid-1956)	Biscuit, Tan, Grey or Red
Claret (from Jan 1957)	Red or Maroon
Cornish Grey (from 1957)	Red, Dark Blue, Light Blue or Grey
Cotswold Blue (from Jan 1957)	Dark Blue or Grey
Cream	Dark Blue, Light Blue or Red
Dove Grey (to 1957)	Biscuit or Tan
Forest Green (from Nov 1957)	Suede Green or Grey
Imperial Maroon (from Jan 57)	Red, Maroon or Biscuit
Indigo Blue (from Jan 1957)	Dark Blue, Light Blue or Grey
Lavender Grey (to 1957)	Dark Blue, Light Blue, Grey, Red or Suede Green
Maroon (mid-1956 to Dec '57)	Biscuit, Tan, or Red
Mist Grey	Red, Dark Blue, Light Blue or Grey
Pacific Blue (from mid-1956)	Dark Blue, Light Blue or Grey
Pastel Blue (to 1957)	Dark Blue or Light Blue
Pastel Green (to 1957 only)	Suede Green or Grey
Pearl Grey (from mid-1956)	Dark Blue, Light Blue, Grey or Red
Sherwood Green (from Jan 1957)	Suede Green or Tan
Suede Green	Suede Green

(*) Initially export colour only, to order.

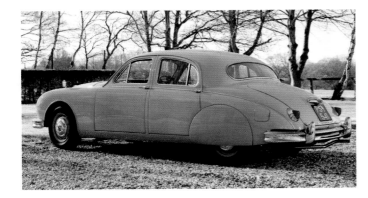

Compared to other models, there was a somewhat limited range of colour schemes for the Mk 1. The trend was towards sombre colour schemes, particularly for the UK market, so many were produced in blacks and greys. Pastel Blue with matching Blue upholstery was a rare but attractive combination, seen here on Michael Bing's 2.4 litre model.

Pearl Grey was a very popular colour with the Mk 1 and early Mk 2 models. This is it on a later 2.4 litre Mk 1 with full spats and whitewall tyres, the latter quite unusual for a UK car. (Author.)

This is the way most Mk 1s were seen in their heyday, without wheel rimbellishers and in one of the many grey paint schemes available; in this case, the colour is Lavender. (Author.)

Maroon was another attractive colour, and in various hues (later known as Imperial Maroon) remained a production colour for Jaguars for many years. (Author.)

Mk 2 and Daimler 2.5 litre V8 Colour Schemes

Exterior	Interior
Black	Red, Grey or Tan; plus Light Tan from late 1960
Carmen Red	Red
Cotswold Blue (to 1966)	Light Blue, Dark Blue or Grey
Cream (to 1960)	Red, Light Blue or Dark Blue
Dark Blue (from Jan 1965)	Light Blue, Dark Blue or Red
Dove Grey (1966 only)	Red, Tan or Grey
Honey Beige (from 1966)	Red or Tan
Indigo Blue (to Dec 1964)	Light Blue, Dark Blue or Red
Mist Grey (to 1966)	Red, Light Blue, Dark Blue or Grey; plus Maroon from late 1960
Old English White (1960 to 1967)	Light Blue, Dark Blue, Grey or Red
Opalescent Blue (dark) (1961 to 1966)	Light Blue, Grey or Red
Opalescent Bronze (1961 to 1962 only)	Suede Green, Tan, Red or Beige
Opalescent Dark Green	Suede Green or Tan
Opalescent Golden Sand (from 1962)	Light Tan or Red
Opalescent Gunmetal Grey (1961 to 1966)	Red, Light Blue, Dark Blue, Beige or Grey
Opalescent Maroon	Maroon or Beige
Opalescent Silver Blue (from 1961)	Dark Blue or Grey; plus Black from 1962
Opalescent Silver Grey (from 1961)	Red, Light Blue, Dark Blue or Grey; plus Black from 1962
Pearl Grey (to 1966)	Red, Light Blue, Dark Blue or Grey
Primrose (from Dec 1964)	Red, Tan or Black
Sherwood Green (to 1967)	Tan or Suede Green; plus Light Tan from 1962
Warwick Grey (from 1964)	Red or Tan
Willow Green (from 1963)	Suede Green, Black or Champagne

Cotswold Blue is a colour more associated with the 1950s and the Mk 1, yet it was still available on the Mk 2 for some time.

Opalescent was the descriptive name given to a new range of metallic paint finishes on Jaguar models in the 1960s. This car is finished in Opalescent Silver Blue, a striking colour even today.

Two variants of the metallic Opalescent Grey were available, Silver Grey as depicted here and a darker Gunmetal.

Carmen Red is probably the most popular colour for a 3.8 litre Mk 2 today, and many restored cars have been changed to this colour from others. With chromed wire wheels it makes a stunningly beautiful car, although the colour was not that popular in the 1960s!

240, 340 and V8-250 Colour Schemes

Ascot Fawn	Black or Red
Black (from July 1968)	Red, Dark Blue or Beige
British Racing Green	Green, Black or Beige
Honey Beige	Black or Red
Indigo Blue	Black, Red or Dark Blue
Old English White (to July 1968)	Black or Red
Powder Blue (from July 1968)	Black, Red or Dark Blue
Primrose	Black
Regency Red	Red or Beige
Sable	Black, Red or Beige
Signal Red (to July 1968)	Black, Red or Beige
Warwick Grey	Black, Red or Dark Blue
White (from July 1968)	Black or Red
Willow Green	Green or Black

Regency was a 'classy' colour for the later cars, seemingly very popular on 340s and Daimler V8-250s as well as S-types and 420s.

S-type Colour Schemes

Black (from 1968)	Beige, Black, Blue or Red
British Racing Green (from 1964)	Suede Green, Tan or Champagne; plus Light Tan from 1967; then Blue or Black only from 1968
Carmen Red (to 1967)	Black (Beige from 1964) or Red
Cotswold Blue (to 1964)	Dark Blue or Grey
Cream (from 1964)	Red, Light Blue or Dark Blue; then Beige, Black, Blue or Red from 1968
Dark Blue (from 1964)	Grey, Light Blue or Red; then Beige, Black, Blue or Red from 1968
Dove Grey (to 1964)	Red, Tan or Grey
Honey Beige (from 1966)	Red or Tan; Beige, Black, Blue or Red from 1968
Imperial Maroon (to 1964)	Red
Old English White (to 1968)	Red or Tan
Opalescent Blue (dark) (to 1964)	Dark Blue, Light Blue, Grey or Red
Opalescent Bronze (to 1964)	Red or Tan
Opalescent Dark Green (to 1967)	Suede Green, Tan or Champagne, plus Beige from 1964
Opalescent Golden Sand (1964 to 67)	Light Tan or Red
Opalescent Gunmetal Grey (to 1964)	Red or Tan
Opalescent Maroon (1964 to 67)	Maroon or Beige
Opalescent Silver Blue (to 1967)	Dark Blue, Light Blue to 1964; Grey or Red from 1964
Opalescent Silver Grey (to 1967)	Red, Grey or Tan
Pearl Grey (to 1964)	Red, Light Blue, Dark Blue or Grey
Pure White (Police white) (*)	Black or Dark Blue
Sherwood Green (to 1967)	Tan or Suede Green, plus Light Tan from 1964
Warwick Grey (from 1964)	Red or Tan; Dark Blue, Light Blue or Tan from 1967; then Beige, Blue, Black or Red from 1968
Willow Green (from 1967/68)	Suede Green, Beige, Grey or Light Tan
(*) Special order only, from 1967.	

Jaguar has never been without a dark green in its colour palette, and this was British Racing Green, which in itself has seen many changes in hue over the years.

Another of Jaguar's 1960s Opalescent colours was Golden Sand. A very popular colour for the more expensive models, like most of the Opalescent paints it did suffer from oxidation over time.

Old English White was always a popular colour, although it never suited the Jaguar saloons as much as the sports cars. This S-type is one of the later versions without the fitted fog lamps.

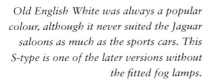

420 and Sovereign Colour Schemes

Ascot Fawn (from 1968)	Beige, Cinnamon, or Suede Green
Black	Red, Grey, Light Tan or Tan; Cinnamon, Red or Grey from 1968
British Racing Green	Suede Green, Beige, Light Tan or Tan (both replaced by Cinnamon from 1968)
Cream	Light Blue, Dark Blue or Red
Dark Blue	Grey, Light Blue or Red
Honey Beige (to 1968)	Red, Light Tan, Tan, Suede Green
Imperial Maroon (to 1968)	Beige or Maroon
Light Blue (from 1968)	Dark Blue, Light Blue or Grey
Opalescent Golden Sand (to 1968)	Red or Light Tan
Opalescent Silver Blue (to 1968)	Dark Blue or Grey
Opalescent Silver Grey (to 1968)	Dark Blue, Light Blue Grey (replaced by Cinnamon in 1968) or Red
Regency Red (from 1968)	Beige or Grey
Sable (from 1968)	Beige, Cinnamon of Grey
Warwick Grey	Dark Blue, Light Tan or Red
Willow Green	Suede Green, Beige, Grey or Light Tan (replaced by Cinnamon in 1968)

NUMBERS BUILT AND IDENTIFICATION

Numbers Built and Identification

Production by year and model

	1955	1956	1957	1958	1959	1960	1961	1962	1963	1964	1965	1966	1967	1968	1969	Totals
2.4 litre	32	8029	3984	4441	3219											19,705
3.4 litre			4536	7164	5580											17,280
2.4 Mk 2					1119	6717	6459	3358	2857	1904	1355	1592	961			26,322
3.4 Mk 2					748	5284	6050	4660	4155	3539	2091	1454	1550			29,531
3.8 Mk 2					665	5534	8727	4725	3241	2631	1401	689	235			27,848
2.5 V8								8	2444	3969	3430	2200	967			13,018
3.4 S									1	2169	3825	2575	646	712		9928
3.8 S									42	4863	5916	3685	362	197		15,065
420												1350	5512	3374		10,236
Sov'n												422	2210	2151	1041	5824
240													911	2867	692	4470
340													1005	1799		2804
V8-250													803	2871	1223	4897
													Grand Total			**186,928**
% (*)		61%	62%	60%	61%	75%	84%	53%	53%	73%	67%	60%	69%	59%	11%	

(*) Percentage of total Jaguar production, by year.

Vehicle Chassis and Engine Numbers

	RHD, from	LHD, from	Engine numbers, from
2.4 litre Mk 1	900001	940001	BB.1001
			BC.1001
			BE.1001
3.4 litre Mk 1	970001	985001	KE.1001
			KF.1001
2.4 litre Mk 2	100001	125001	BG.1001
			BH.1001
			BJ.1001
3.4 litre Mk 2	150001	175001	KG.1001
			KH.1001
			KJ.1001
3.8 litre Mk 2	200001	210001	LA.1001
			LB.1001
			LC.1001
			LE.1001
240	1J.1001	1J.30001	7J.1001
340	1J.50001	1J.80001	7J.10001
3.4 litre S-type	1B.1001	1B.25001	7B.1001
3.8 litre S-type	1B.50001	1B.75001	7B.50001
420 and Sovereign	1F.1001	1F.25001	7F.1001
2.5 litre V8 (Daimler)	1A.1001	1A.20001	7A.1001
V8-250 (Daimler)	1K.1001	1K.30001	7K.1001

Notes:

• A DN suffix to a chassis number denotes a car fitted with overdrive.

• A BW suffix to a chassis number denotes a car fitted with automatic transmission.

• A -7, -8, or –9 to an engine number denotes the compression ratio.

Identification

Chassis and Body numbers

The car's chassis number is always stamped on a vehicle identification plate, which for most models was attached to the left-hand (carburettor) side inner wing area, near the top. For certain later models (because of the fitment of different ancillaries) and on all Daimler V8 cars, this plate was situated on the exhaust manifold side inner wing area.

All the cars carry their chassis number embossed into the front panel behind the radiator grille, and this is accessible when the bonnet is open.

Engine numbers

The engine number is always stamped on the cylinder block above the oil filter and at the front of the cylinder head casting.

Gearbox numbers

The prefix GB was used for the gearboxes of 2.4 litre, 3.4 litre and early Mk 2 models without overdrive. The designation GBN (the suffix N always denoting suitable for overdrive) is for the same gearbox when fitted with the Laycock de Normanville overdrive unit.

The serial number is on the top cover, stamped around a large circular ring. It should also be stamped on the left-hand side of the main casing in the top rear corner. A suffix of CR, J or MS will indicate the fitment of close-ratio gearing.

Registrations

For cars registered in the United Kingdom, registration numbers were issued by local council authorities, and each authority had its own distinctive letter allocations. Until 1963, single, double or triple alphabetical identification was preceded or followed by a series of numerical digits. Examples of this would be:

1352 E, 234 RVA, TNU 123. The last one or two letters identified the local area of registration; in these cases
E = Staffordshire
VA = Lanarkshire, and
NU = Derbyshire.

To maximise the available registrations available for a county council, when the limit of 999 was reached, the order of numbers and letters reversed, so that TNU 123 would eventually become 123 TNU.

From 1963 a new system was adopted with a further letter to identify the actual registration period. So, for the cars in this book, from their original period, the age related registration letters were

A   1963
B   1964
C   1965
D   1966
E   January to July 1967
F   August 1967 to July 1968
G   August 1968 to July 1969
H   August 1969 to July 1970

An example of an age-related plate would be NVT 394F (VT indicating Stoke on Trent registration and the F representing the later months of 1967 or the first part of 1968).

A good way to identify the true age of a vehicle (if the door glasses have not been changed) is to read the detailing etched into each glass. A dot appears underneath a letter in the word 'Toughened'. As marked here, the dot is under the letter 'D' (the ninth letter), so the car was fitted up with glass in a year ending in a 9 – in the case of this 240, 1969.

On all the models featured in this publication the chassis number is stamped into the front panel as you open the bonnet.

Complete identification plates are fitted to all cars, usually on the inner wing under the bonnet or on the bulkhead behind the engine. There will also be a Jaguar Cars identification plate in the same area.

PRODUCTION CHANGES

The following information is taken from Jaguar's own written records, with some inevitable cross-overs between models.

2.4 litre and 3.4 litre Mk 1 production changes

For a key to chassis and engine number sequences, please see the preceding section on Numbers Built and Identification.

Date	RHD change point	LHD change point	Other change point	Change
1955	900207	94004 [sic]		Spare wheel clamp modified with better shaping to improve strength. (Part No BD11007 replaced BD10636.)
December 1955			Engine BB.1001	Cylinder heads modified with reduced depth of tapped holes for the studs on the inner face.
	900351	940020		Choke indicator plate on the dashboard now with revised lettering, common to that used on other Jaguar models at the time.
	900351	940020		Front road springs changed, the new ones being ⅜ inch longer (Part No C.8924/1 replacing C.8924).
May 1956	900522	940200		Brake master cylinder and reservoir altered, affecting the angle at which the reservoir was attached to the cylinder in relation to the mounting studs. The earlier type had a reservoir filler cap in front of the cylinder; this later type had the cap situated to the right of the cylinder (Part No C.12184 replaced C.8955).
April 1956	900822	940207		Heater intake duct shaping altered to provide a straighter run for the rev counter cable. Existing cars with the old ducting were modified by creating an indentation in the ducting.
	900822	940207		The 25mm choke tube in the Solex carburettors was replaced by one of 24mm, air correction jets were changed from 160 to 180, and 1.5mm needle vales for 2.0mm.
				New paint options added: Pearl Grey, Pacific Blue, Carmine Red, Arbor Green and Maroon.
	900864	940210		Securing bolts to the drive gear in the differential case increased in size from ¼in to 7/16in.
May 1956				Dealers asked to add extra welding to the Panhard rod mountings for strength; these mountings had been prone to cracking and breakage. The same modification was now adopted by the factory on cars before despatch (with no new part numbers).
June 1956	901582	940606		Rear axle ratio on non-overdrive models changed from 4.55 to 1 to 4.27 to 1.
				Stronger clutch pedal retaining spring fitted, with a revised spring plate and shakeproof washer. The modification came from the then current Mark VIIM model.

Date	RHD change point	LHD change point	Other change point	Change
	901482	940560		Modified type of speedometer cable fitted, now with a fluted inner cable and nylon insert. A modified speedometer drive incorporating a lip-type rubber seal prevented any seepage travelling up the cable. (These change numbers for non-overdrive cars.)
	901561	940580		Modified speedometer cable and drive, as above. (These numbers for cars with overdrive.)
			Engine BB.2500	Metalastic vibration damper was fitted to the front end of the crankshaft.
July 1956	903163	941252		Overdrive cars now fitted with a close-ratio gearbox (Part No BB.5691).
	902169	940973		Revised type of coil spring rear engine mounting. (Part Nos C.12298 for non-overdrive and C.12299 for overdrive models).
	902169	940973		Revised rear road spring mounting plate with a one-piece pressing introduced (Part No C.12343).
September 1956			Engine BB.3118	New type of Solex carburetor, incorporating a weir in the float chamber.
				Ignition static timing on 8:1 compression engines altered from 10 degrees to 6 degrees BTDC
			Engine BB.5024	Copper washers fitted to the sump strainer cover plate.
	902882	941156		Modified rear springs with synthetic rubber to the ends of the spring leaves, eliminating a reported 'cracking' noise.
October 1956	904285	941631		Modified dampers (Part Nos C.8924 front and C.8926 rear).
November 1956	905610	941767		Shroud added to scuttle ventilator to prevent water ingress behind the instrument panel.
			Engine BB.7113	Carburettor main jets changed to size 110 (from 115).
			Engine BB.9001	Pressed steel sump (Part No C.9155) replaced the earlier aluminium type. Engine oil dipstick now with a knurled level section to aid the checking of oil.
January 1957	906247	941930		Check valve fitted between the inlet manifold and the brake servo, attached to the inlet manifold studs (Part No C.12790).
				Paint colours for 2.4 litre changed: Maroon re-named Imperial Maroon because of a new paint formula being used. Claret, Sherwood Green, Indigo Blue and Cotswold Blue added to the range.
February 1957	906500	941985		High setting to the hydraulic dampers now adopted.
			Engine BB.9657	Camshafts modified with a hole drilled through the base of each into the main oilway to reduce tappet noise (Part Nos C.13082 inlet and C.13083 exhaust).
				Rear upper spring mountings now had extra welded support brackets.
May 1957	906964	942182		New style of coolant radiator with separate filler and inlet pipe (as fitted to the new 3.4 litre cars).
	906949	942190		RB310 voltage regulator (Part No C.8821) replaced the earlier RB106.
				Soon after production started, 3.4 litre engines changed from LB carburettor needles to LB1 needles.
		985600		Slightly modified radiator grille with five instead of four fixing studs.
July 1957			Engines BC.2256 (2.4)	Modified oil filter with a dome nut to retain the oil pressure relief valve KE.3054 (3.4) and with a straight outlet adaptor for the base to the sump. Also modified blanking plate with a dimple.
	907359 970327	942311 986134		Strengthened windscreen wiper motor (Part Nos C.13503 RHD and C.13504 LHD).

Date	RHD change point	LHD change point	Other change point	Change
September 1957			Engines BC.2959 (2.4) KE.3888 (3.4)	Smaller dynamo pulley to increase rotational speed, together with a shortened fan belt. Air cleaner now added to the air intake of the 6⅞in brake servo.
	907974	942465		Larger 3.4 litre style radiator grille now fitted to all cars. Front wings and intake modified appropriately on 2.4-litre models. Jaguar thereafter made available front wing repair panels so that in the event of damage, earlier cars could be modified to the later style grille.
			Engine BC.3161	Glass bowl type petrol filter now fitted, with a gauze (Part No C.13681).
			Engine KE.3025	More efficient anti-creep solenoid (Part No C.12750) for automatic transmission models. Longer inlet valve guides (1 13/16in instead of 1½in) now fitted to all engines.
	970877	986554		Extra baffles added to the exhaust silencers to eliminate noise.
	971637	987293		Modified oil bath air cleaner. Carburettor needles changed from TL to SC type. Interior rear view mirror re-positioned from the dashboard top rail to the roof area.
November 1957				Automatic transmission became an option on the 2.4 litre models. New Suede Green interior trim added to the range.
			Engines BC.3600 (2.4) KE.4856 (3.4)	Revised type of oil pressure relief valve, with a stop pin fitted to the centre of the spring to limit valve travel.
			Engines BC.3699 (2.4) KE.4964 (3.4)	Synthetic rubber bonded chain dampers replaced the previous nylon type.
	908095 970048	942483 986592		5½in brake servo with an adjustable type pushrod now fitted to drum-braked cars only
	971503	987132		Exhaust downpipes shortened by 2in and the pipes ahead of the silencers lengthened by the same amount.
January 1958				New paint colour (Forest Green) added to the range.
			Engines BC.4408 (2.4) KE.5733 (3.4)	Bore in the outlet pipe of the thermostat housing increased by 25mm to accommodate a modified thermostat (Part No C.13944).
February 1958	909061 971732	942677 987406		Drum-braked cars now fitted with a larger 6⅞in brake servo; brake pedal and clutch pedal mounting changed to suit.
	909636 972037	942729 987685		Progressive bump stops added to the front suspension.
	911118 972401	942854 988216		Modified inner pad carrier and lever now available to prevent handbrake cross cables fouling the rear wheelarches
April 1958				Dunlop RS4 tyres replaced RS3s as the factory fit on 3.4 litre cars.
May 1958				New type of rear road spring (Part No C.10791/1) for all cars, giving a change in free camber.
			Engine KE.7052 (3.4)	Valve block in automatic transmissions modified to eliminate jerk on a closed throttle downshift between gears.
July 1958				Metal toggle overdrive switch on the dashboard replaced the earlier plastic illuminated type.
				60-watt headlamp bulbs introduced on all RHD models.
	911958	943149		New style of oil bath air cleaner (Part No C.14213), fitted to the cylinder head with a pipe running forward for the air intake.
November 1958	911522 973987	943124 989137		Modified Girling hydraulic dampers (C.14586) fitted to the front of all cars.
	912637 975162	943900 990178		Modified Girling hydraulic dampers (C.14587) fitted to the rear of all cars.

Date	RHD change point	LHD change point	Other change point	Change
	915349	943118		Revised attachment for the rear caliper adaptor plate on drum brakes, with longer bolts, self-locking nuts and shakeproof washers.
				12-bladed engine cooling fan with appropriate fan cowl now fitted to 2.4 models (Part Nos C12391 fan, and C14732 shield).
January 1959	913144 975688	943331 990694		Dunlop bridge-type brake calipers with quick change pads adopted for disc-wheeled cars.
	913234 975783	943343 990795		Dunlop bridge-type brake calipers with quick change pads adopted for wire-wheeled cars
				75-spoke wire wheels replaced the 60-spoke type for all models. German market examples from then on had to be fitted with non-eared knock-on hubs.
			Engines BC.8075 (2.4) KF.2501 (3.4)	Vacuum reservoir incorporated in line between the inlet manifold and the servo. Reservoir tank fitted underneath the right-hand front wing, forward of the wheel. Check valve also fitted, with a hose from the inlet manifold to the longer check valve connection and another hose to the servo.
				Modified ball joints for all cars, with a larger diameter bolt and increased angle of movement.
	912622	943267		On drum-braked cars, ball joint hole centres in the upper wishbone levers and packing pieces increased from 1 11/16in to 1¾in.
	912744 975232	943288 990270		On disc-braked cars, ball joint hole centres in the upper wishbone levers and packing pieces increased from 1 11/16in to 1¾in.
				60-watt headlamp bulbs now standardised on all cars.
			Engine KF.2501 (3.4)	½in fan belt for 3.4 engines, with appropriately modified pulleys.
April 1959	914564 976917	943496 991866		Re-designed steering box (Part Nos C.14845 RHD and C.14846 LHD), with lower gearing, giving 4¼ turns lock to lock; also new idler assembly (C.14887).
			Engines BE.1116 (2.4) KF.6219 (3.4)	Lead-indium big end bearings now fitted.
May 1959				Oil filter blanking plate now no longer used.
	913953 977762	943437 992494		25-amp (C.45 PVS 6) dynamo and replacement regulator now fitted.
				Electrically driven rev counter replaced the cable driven type, as with other Jaguar models of this period.

2.4 litre, 3.4 litre and 3.8 litre Mk 2 production changes

For a key to chassis and engine number sequences, please see the preceding section on Numbers Built and Identification.

Date	RHD change point	LHD change point	Other change point	Change
January 1960				Tailpipes now clipped to silencers for ease of removal and replacement (they were welded on the first 200 cars produced).
March 1960	101446 151003 200668	125370 175499 211867		A recalibrated 60psi oil pressure gauge replaced the previous 100psi gauge as owners expressed concern at the readings. This required a replacement oil pressure sensor and subsequently a replacement kit was provided free of charge by Jaguar to dealerships for those owners who had complained.
			Engines KG.1891 (3.4) LA.2330 (3.8)	A notched fan belt was fitted.
April 1960	100731 150562 200301	125269 175082 211042		The steering column stalks were reversed (overdrive and auto to the right and indicators to the left).
	100731 150562 200301	125269 175082 211042		The original oil bath type of air cleaner was replaced by a conventional pancake type.
				The engine breather was altered, venting to the carburettors.
				Longer front springs (by ⅛in) were fitted to all models.
July 1960				A water valve was fitted within the heater system, actuated from the temperature control on the centre console.
				Black figured Rexine replaced the painted matt black finish on the centre dash panel.
				A breather pipe was added to the fuel tank and a non-vented fuel filler cap was fitted.
September 1960	103669 152282 201798	125711 176024 213964		5J disc road wheels replaced the earlier 4½J type.
				Power-assisted steering became an extra cost option for all models.
				A 4HA differential was standardised on all models (previously only fitted to cars with 3.4 and 3.8 litre engines), and the propshaft was modified appropriately.
November 1960				The steering column mounting was marginally lowered.
				An organ type accelerator pedal replaced the pendant type.
				A spring-loaded hinge was fitted to the centre console ashtray.
				Flexible sun visors replaced the board-backed flush fitting type.
				The chromed brass door window frames were modified with strengthening sections welded in at waist height to eliminate flexing and cracking. This necessitated small cut-outs in the wood finishers to the door trims.
			Engines KG.4104 (3.4) LA.7214 (3.8)	An SU fuel pump was fitted, with a revised siting for the oil filter (facing downwards).
				Plastic brake fluid reservoir replaced the metal type.
				Boss for Bray electric sump heater moved from the left-hand side to the right-hand side on all engines.
January 1961				Crankshaft rear seal now fitted to all engines.
February 1961				Forged wishbones replaced the steel type on all models.
				Stronger anti-roll bar fitted to all models.
				Opalescent exterior paint finishes added to the range: Dark Blue, Blue, Gunmetal, Silver, Silver Blue and Bronze.

Date	RHD change point	LHD change point	Other change point	Change
			Engines KG.5366 (3.4) LA.8593 (3.8)	Dipstick tube added
June 1961			Engines BG.9498 (2.4) KG.6738 (3.4) LB.1850 (3.8)	Modified oil sump, to accommodate a larger oil pump (Part Nos C.17645 and C.17655).
				Modified fuel pump with a shorter cell housing.
	105629 153583 202910	126080 176602 215650		Toughened windscreen now fitted, with a zoned area on the driver's side.
				Rubber buffers now fitted to the rear edges of the front wings to meet the bonnet when closed. Others added to the outer rear edges of the front and rear sill areas to meet the doors when closed.
				Cast iron brake cylinder blocks replaced the malleable iron type. These had modified self-adjusting mechanisms without spring washers, and were of integral construction with no end plate.
	155965 205364	177304 217573		Extended type of automatic transmission dipstick now fitted.
				A modified shallow radiator filler cap and neck now fitted, to aid cooling.
August 1961			Engines KG.9884 (3.4) LA.5312 (3.8)	Inlet camshafts now drilled to give silent running. The same modification was made later in the year to 2.4 litre engines from BH.2900.
	108998 156343 205633	126479 177360 217969		Water deflectors now fitted to the front hubs.
				Self-adjusting handbrake mechanisms now fitted to all models.
				Rubber sealing strips now fitted to the front edge of the doors.
October 1961			Engines BH.4551 (2.4) KH 2794 (3.4) LB.8247 (3.8)	Spring-loaded jockey pulley now fitted to adjust the fan belt tension automatically.
			Engines KH 2794 (3.4) LB.8247 (3.8)	Crankshaft rear end cover modified to take an asbestos rope oil seal.
			Engines BH.4553 (2.4) KH.2794 (3.4) LB.8359 (3.8)	Modified camshaft cover was fitted on the exhaust side.
January 1962	111418 158371 207313	126652 177753 219801		Front seat belt anchorages now fitted to all bodies.
				Front seat belt anchorages now fitted to all bodies.
February 1962				High-output C42 dynamo for 3.4 litre and 3.8 litre models.
				Modified sealing rings of steel and asbestos now fitted between the exhaust manifolds and downpipes on 3.4 litre and 3.8 litre models.
March 1962			Engine BH.5336	Modified fan belt for 2.4 litre engines (Part No C.19523), bringing modifications to the dynamo, crankshaft and water pump pulleys.
			Engines BH.5853 (2.4) KH.4020 (3.4) LC.1506 (3.8)	Slightly modified sump (Part No C.19922).l
April 1962				Modified brake servo incorporating a two-stage air valve (Part No C.19612) on all cars.
				The fan belt modification from March for 2.4 litre models was now fitted to all engines.

Date	RHD change point	LHD change point	Other change point	Change
September 1962				Brico Maxiflex scraper rings now fitted to 3.8 litre engines in the hope of reducing oil consumption.
	112995 160201 208535			All RHD cars now equipped with sealed-beam headlights.
			Engines BH.7969 (2.4) KH.7063 (3.4) LC.4265 (3.8)	Oil filter mounting modified with five fixing bolts instead of four; rubber seal added to the oil pressure relief valve and balance valve.
			Engines BH.7671 (2.4) KH.7310 (3.4) LC.4461 (3.8)	Longer handle for oil level dipstick.
November 1962	114063 161400 209382	126900 178733 221881		Upper steering column modified to accept an optional extra Waso combined ignition and steering wheel lock.
January 1963	114110 161442 209424			Reinforcement bracket added to the Panhard rod mounting and nylon washers fitted to the top and bottom wheel swivels and tie rod seals.
				Taper roller bearings now fitted to the steering idler assembly.
February 1963				Stiffer Girling dampers for all models.
March 1963			Engines BH.8488 (2.4) KH.7999 (3.4)	Maxiflex compression rings now fitted to 2.4 litre and 3.4 litre engines, as already done on 3.8 litre engines.
	114849 162488 230140	127055 178974 222241		Lower steering column modified to be the same as on the contemporary Mark X saloon.
				Rears of front seats modified with an extra cut-out to improve rear legroom.
April 1963	114992 162251 230298	127075 179010 222289		Door window frames modified with the addition of flocked rubber inserts.
				Higher output dynamo and C.42 control box now adopted for all cars.
	115185 162955 230496	127126 179116 222524		9lbs radiator pressure cap now fitted in place of the earlier 4lbs type.\
				Rubber dust excluder now fitted to right-hand headlights.
			Engines KJ.1121 (3.4) LC.6993 (3.8)	Improved water pump.
				Larger diameter (3in) propshaft fitted, with sealed-for-life joints.
August 1963				Waterproof rubber caps now fitted to plug and HT leads where they entered the distributor cap.
September 1963				On 3.4 and 3.8 litre engines, the plug leads were increased in length to permit a revised run of the cables over the cam covers.
October 1963				7lbs radiator pressure cap now fitted to all cars.
				Revised front suspension cross member mounting (Part No C.23314), with improved bonding; identifiable by a small cross moulded in rubber.
	116114 164002 231586	127312 179499 353182		Revised Mk X-style steering wheel now fitted to all models; on early cars this did not feature the 'live' centre horn push.
November 1963				Rectifier added to the electric time clock mounted in the rev counter.
			Engines BH.7671 (2.4) KH.7310 (3.4) LC.4461 (3.8)	Oil level dipstick re-designed with extra markings.
January 1964				Grease nipples fitted to front wheel bearings on cars fitted with disc wheels.

Date	RHD change point	LHD change point	Other change point	Change
March 1964	116999 165424 231931	127430 179656 223349		Reshaped wooden panel for the B/C posts, to mount the interior courtesy lights.
				3.8 litre engines received revised pistons with chamfer and drain hole below the piston oil control rings.
April 1964			Engines KJ.4037 (3.4) LC.8900 (3.8)	Flywheels now standardised with the S-type models.
May 1964	117502 166390 232536	127509 179795 223530		4lbs radiator pressure cap reintroduced as standard.
				New SU fuel pump standardised with S-type models.
				8-amp fuse for the intermediate speed hold and overdrive switches standardised with S-type models.
	117556 164495 231603	127334 179522 223125		Revised fixing rod for the vacuum reservoir brackets.
June 1964				Revised brake bleed nipples (repositioned from the outside to the inside of each caliper), with hydraulic pipes modified to suit.
August 1964			Engines BJ.3662 (2.4) KJ.5520 (3.4) LE.1218 (3.8)	The engine lifting brackets were fitted over longer cylinder head studs and there was also a modified spark plug conduit.
				Modified timing chain cover allowed the front oil seal to be replaced without removing the cover.
	117269 to 117555 165960 to 166510 232770 to 232600	127465 to 127519 179701 to 179830 223428 to 223584		PVC heel pads fitted to the front floor carpets of these Chassis Number ranges only.
October 1964			Engines BJ.3535 (2.4) KJ.5520 (3.4) LE.1214 (3.8)	All engines now fitted with the same sump as S-type models, to standardise production (Part No C.24502).
	117901 167287 233039	127605 179943 223837		Automatic transmission cars now no longer had a chromed 'automatic' emblem on the boot lid.
				Shields added to the inside of brake discs.
				Upper universal joint added to steering column.
December 1964				Paint finishes Warwick Grey, Indigo Blue and Primrose added to range.
	118268 167989 233460	127679 180035 224023		Larger radiator block (Part No C.24916), with revised fan cowling (Part No C.24965).
January 1965				Radio aperture finisher panel on the centre console amended with relocated studs at 6¼in centres instead of 5 7/16in.
April 1965	118867 168957 233919	127760 180137 224086		Longer water drain tube from the battery tray.
				Lucas 5SJ screen washer system now fitted, with a reservoir in high-density polythene instead of glass. The system operation changed so that the wash was only active as long as the dashboard switch was held in the up (on) position.
June 1965			Engines BJ.4484 (2.4) KJ.6898 (3.4) LE.2047 (3.8)	Waterproof cover added to the distributor cap.
				A revised style of gauze was fitted to the scuttle ventilator.
			Engines BJ.4609 (2.4) KJ.7071 (3.4) LE.2123 (3.8)	Oil filler caps now with a rubber O-ring in place of the earlier fibre type.

Date	RHD change point	LHD change point	Other change point	Change
				Automatic transmission torque converter modified to improve shift quality, and a P suffix added to the gearbox serial numbers where applicable (Part No C.25615).
September 1965				Hazard warning light system added to export models as standard equipment.
	119200 169341 234125	127822 180188 224150		All-synchromesh four-speed manual gearbox similar to that already used in Mark X and S-type models standardised (Part No C.25867). This brought a revised diaphragm clutch and self-adjusting slave cylinder, clutch fork return spring and clutch housing.
November 1965				Paper element oil filters now fitted to all cars.
				Front quarter-lights modified to provide an extra 'notch' opening. Rear quarter-light pivot screws also Loctited in position to prevent them working loose.
March 1966	119356 169632 234395	127868 180262 224207		Handbrake mechanism retraction plates redesigned to improve alignment of the pad carriers.
April 1966				Black exterior paint added to the standard range.
	119581 170091 234715	127912 180310 224271		Direction indicator switch on the steering column redesigned with a nylon striker ring which required less movement of the stalk to engage.
				Direction indicator switch on the steering column redesigned with a nylon striker ring which required less movement of the stalk to engage.
				Lucas 9H horns replaced the older type 618U.
	119902 170565 235046	127998 180398 224417		Heated rear screens (when fitted) now with a dash-mounted on-off switch and warning light.
September 1966				Ambla upholstery standardised on all models and leather became an extra cost option. Occasional tables deleted from the front seat backs with both Ambla and leather upholstery. Tufted carpets replaced the pile type.
				Headlining and sun visors standardised with S-type models.
				Foglamps deleted as standard equipment and replaced by mock horn grilles. The legend on the dashboard lighting switch also changed, as the F identification was removed.
				Revised door window waist chromes with rubber seal inserts replaced the earlier weather strips.
				The chromed waist trim finisher and vertical chrome finisher on the B/C post were now a single–piece pressing.
December 1966	120291	128054		Exhaust tailpipes on 2.4 litre cars modified with a separate chromed portion, as on the 3.4 and 3.8 litre models.
	170881 235152	180474 224156		Tailpipes now detachable and secured by self-tapping screws.
			Engine BJ.6132 (2.4)	Crankshaft vibration damper redesigned with an integral fan belt pulley.
				Revised brake fluid warning light on all models, and a moulded rubber cover over the electrical connections on the reservoir.
March 1967				Standard paint range now with five metallic and seven non-metallic options. The metallics were Opalescent Silver Blue, Silver Grey, Maroon, Dark Green and Golden Sand; the non-metallics were Primrose, Indigo Blue, Carmen Red, Willow Green, Warwick Grey, Black and Honey Beige.
	171101 235196	180529 224588		Varamatic power steering system from the S-type adopted for 3.4 litre and 3.8 litre cars.
			Engines BJ.5736 (2.4) KJ.8772 (3.4) LE.3443 (3.8)	Oil seals now fitted to the inlet guides.
				Hazard warning light systems on US market cars now had 35-amp fuses instead of 25-amp types.

Date	RHD change point	LHD change point	Other change point	Change
July 1967				420G style chromed hub caps replaced the earlier type on all models.
				Boot lock modified to improve the latch system.
				Velcro nylon strips replaced carpet fastenings on all cars.

240 and 340 production changes

For a key to chassis and engine number sequences, please see the preceding section on Numbers Built and Identification.

Date	RHD change point	LHD change point	Other change point	Change
January 1968	1J.1429 1J.50480	1J.30013 1J.80071		Removable element replaced the filter gauze in the petrol feed line filter.
July 1968				Three new exterior paint finishes: Powder Blue, Black, and White. Signal Red dropped from the range.
	1J.1398 1J.50452	1J.30043 1J.80094		Non-eared knock-on hub caps for wire-wheeled models standardised on cars for Germany, Sweden, Denmark, Switzerland and Japan. Also cylinder block heaters became standard equipment on cars for Canada.
				Improved crankshaft front oil seal (Part No C.24611/1) fitted to all engines.
				On cars destined for Germany, the headlamp units now had integral sidelights. The separate wing-mounted sidelights remained in place but were not wired up.
	1J.2037 1J.5118	1J.30225 1J.80222		Differently calibrated dashboard water temperature gauge, with zoned markings for 'NORMAL' and 'DANGER'. (This became the standard type supplied by the Jaguar Parts Department as stocks of the older type ran out.)
			Engines 7J.1891 (240) 7J.51712 (340)	Modified Lucas ignition coil with push-on terminals.
December 1968	1J.30465	1J.80425		All LHD cars now fitted with standard pattern European headlights (Part No C.21726).
	1J.3432 1J.5241	1J.30571 1J.80536		Revised Lucas starter solenoid (Part No C.30287) replaced earlier type 76776.
				All engines now fitted with sintered valve seat inserts of a reduced depth (Part Nos C.28224 inlet, and C.28225 exhaust.)
				All cars now with a non-hydrostatic clutch slave cylinder that required manual adjustment as the clutch wore.
January 1969				New connecting rod bolts and nuts on all engines for increased tensile strength (Part Nos C.22246 bolts, and C.28535 nuts).
March 1969			Engine 7J.52826 (340)	New clutch unit, with a higher rated diaphragm spring.
				Laycock overdrive units now had a tapered expansion plug in the rear face of the gearbox.
May 1969			Engine 7J.5358 (340)	Modified metallic petrol pipe assembly.

2.5 litre V8 and V8-250 production changes

All body, trim, suspension, steering and brake changes identified for the contemporary Mk 2, 240 and 340 models applied to Daimlers, with the addition of those listed below.

For a key to chassis and engine number sequences, please see the preceding section on Numbers Built and Identification.

Date	Change
January 1964	Rear axle ratio changed from 4.55 to 1 to 4.27 to 1.
April1964	Borg Warner automatic transmission modified to incorporate D1 and D2 selector positions.
January 1965	A limited slip differential became an extra cost option.
February 1967	The Jaguar all-synchromesh four-speed manual gearbox (with or without overdrive) became an option on the Daimler and was accompanied by appropriate trim changes.
	All cars had strengthened engine mountings.
September 1967	From the introduction of the V8-250, the main exterior and trim changes were the same as those for the 240 and 340 models, except that the Daimlers retained leather trim and foglights. Other differences on the Daimlers were: • 420-style hubcaps incorporating the 'D' motif • Revised rear body valance to accommodate the new slim line bumper bars • Reclining front seats standardised • Revised interior door cards with padded top rolls and stained wooden fillets • Ventilated leather upholstery • Marles Varamatic power steering became an option • Alternators (11 AC type) replaced dynamos, and a 4TR control box was fitted.

S-type production changes

For a key to chassis and engine number sequences, please see the preceding section on Numbers Built and Identification.

Date	RHD change point	LHD change point	Other change point	Change
January 1964			Engines 7B.1005 (3.4) 7B.50348 (3.8	Redesigned timing cover with a front oil seal recess.
				Revised pistons with chamfer and drain hole below the piston oil control rings to improve oil circulation, as on all contemporary Jaguar engines.
May 1964	1B.1002 1B.50246	1B.25004 1B.75048		Elastollan upper steering column bearings fitted.
	1B.1004 1B.5032	1B.25005 1B.75053		An 8-amp fuse was added to the intermediate speed hold and overdrive switch circuit.
	1B.1135 1B.50580	1B.25047 1B.75151		A 4lbs pressure radiator cap replaced the 7lbs type.
June 1964				Dunlop SP14 radial tyres replaced the RS crossplies, although Dunlop RS5 tyres were used when whitewalls were specified.
				The distance pieces between the front spring seat and lower wishbone were deleted.
October 1964	1B.52037	1B.76292		An 8in brake servo replaced the 6⅞in type.
				Shields were added to the inside of the brake discs to reduce wear on the inner pads.
				An upper steering column joint was added.
	1B.2192 1B.52078	1B.25301 1B.76310		Jaguar all-synchromesh four-speed manual gearbox replaced the old Moss type, and the rear engine mounting on overdrive models was modified.
December 1964				The petrol tank vent pipe was redesigned in a stiffer material.
				Cars with overdrive received a new speedometer to suit the compact overdrive unit now fitted to all synchromesh gearboxes.

Date	RHD change point	LHD change point	Other change point	Change
	1B.2200 1B.52162	1B.25302 1B.76361		Larger radiator block fitted (Part No C.24916), with accompanying fan cowling (Part No C.24965).
April 1965				Longer water drain tube from the battery tray.
	1B.2769 1B.5990	1B.25382 1B.76922		A nylon thrust bearing replaced the aluminium bronze type on the upper steering column.
				Viton-tipped carburettor needles with black rubber tips were fitted to all engines.
				Rubber valve seals replaced cork washers in the fuel pumps.
June 1965	1B.2998 1B.53183	1B.25430 1B.77221		A Girling brake master cylinder with a smaller diameter main spring replaced the Dunlop type.
				A rubber O-ring replaced the earlier fibre type on all engines.
	1B.3576 1B.53892	1B.25511 1B.77577		Final drive on the 3.54:1 ratio cars now had drive flanges integral with the driveshafts.
	1B.3605 1B.53950	1B.25515 1B.77631		Lucas 5SJ screen washer system fitted, with a high-density polythene reservoir instead of the earlier glass type. The system operation changed so that the wash was only active while the dashboard switch was held in the up (on) position.
	1B.3698 1B.53983	1B.25517 1B.77649		Final drive on the 3.77:1 ratio cars now had drive flanges integral with the driveshafts, matching that on 3.54:1 cars.
	1B.4000	1B.54357		Extra packing pieces were added to the right-hand front spring to equalise standing height.
			Engines 7B.3615 (3.4) 7B.55645 (3.8)	Waterproof cover added to the distributor cap.
			Engines 7B.4921 (3.4) 7B.57695 (3.8)	The plastic rev counter generator driving dog was replaced by a bonded steel and rubber type.
				A Waso combined ignition and steering wheel lock was now available as an extra cost option.
September 1965				A hazard warning light system was added to all export models as standard equipment.
	1B.25633	1B.78204		Tail lamps no longer fused on cars destined for Germany, to meet new legislation.
			Engines 7B.5213 (3.4) 7B.58367 (3.8)	Hydrostatic clutch slave cylinder fitted.
November 1965	1B.4534 1B.54955	1B.25606 1B.78127		Adjustable top bearing added to steering column.
	1B.4607 1B.55057	1B.26515 1B.78160		Rear quarter-light pivot screws now Loctited in position to prevent them working loose. At the same time the front quarter-lights were modified to provide an extra 'notch' opening.
April 1966	1B.5139 1B.55688	1B.25706 1B.78495		Modified front brake caliper assemblies incorporated a bracket and a clip securing the hydraulic pipe from the flexible hose union.
	1B.5302 1B.55836	1B.25777 1B.78835		Modified steering box, with modified inner column and main nut assembly, to provide an interference fit with the lower steering column.
	1B.6092 1B.56872	1B.25788 1B.78909		Indicator switch on the steering column redesigned with a nylon striker ring which required less movement of the stalk.
	1B.6438 1B.57175	1B.25850 1B.79231		Heated rear screen provided with a separate switch and warning light on the dashboard.
			Engines 7B.6572 (3.4) 7B.60391 (3.8	Borg and Beck diaphragm clutch fitted.
December 1966				Brake fluid warning light changed, and a moulded rubber cover added over the electrical connections on the reservoir.

Date	RHD change point	LHD change point	Other change point	Change
	1B.6817 1B.57772	1B.25914 1B.79633		Chromed tailpipe finishers now detachable and with a screw fitment.
				Chromed tailpipe finishers now detachable and with a screw fitment.
			Gearbox JBN.8121	Retaining washer added to the bottom of the gearbox lever to prevent it coming away from the bonded rubber bush.
March 1967			Engines 7B.7090 (3.4) 7B.60959 (3.8)	Circlips fitted to the valve guides.
			Engines 7B.9687 (3.4) 7B.64800 (3.8)	Lock washers replaced plain washers on the main bearing cap bolts.
				On US-market cars, a 35-amp fuse replaced the 25-amp type for the hazard warning light system.
	1B.8324 1B.59210	1B.26208 1B.80265		Laminated windscreen now fitted as standard.
July 1967	1B.8433 1B.59472	1B.26213 1B.80272		Front and rear seat belt anchorage points now fitted as standard.
	1B.8624 1B.59494	1B.26233 1B.80282		Ambla upholstery standardised and leather now an extra-cost option. Mock horn grilles in place of fog lamps, and tufted carpets replaced the pile type.
	1B.8624	1B.26233		Powr-Lok limited slip differential option for 3.4 litre models discontinued.
	1B.8682 1B.59539	1B.26240 1B.80293		Varamatic power-assisted steering system modified.
January 1968	1B.8735 1B.59545	1B.26240 1B.80296		Grease nipples added to the rear halfshafts, replacing the sealed for life type.
	1B.8753 1B.59547	1B.26240 1B.80296		Handbrake lever modified to reduce effort.
	1B.8876 1B.59558	1B.26244 1B.80300		Removable element replaced the filter gauze in the petrol feed line filter.
			Engines 7B.8662 (3.4) 7B.64823 (3.8)	Improved crankshaft damper plate, with all elements in a single assembly.
		1B.26299 1B.80372		Headlamps on cars destined for Germany now with integral side lights. Standard side lights retained but not wired in.
July 1968	1B.9118 1B.59610	1B.26283 1B.80350		Differently calibrated dashboard water temperature gauge, with zoned markings for 'NORMAL' and 'DANGER'. (This became the standard type supplied by the Jaguar Parts Department as stocks of the older type ran out.)
			Engines 7B.10458 (3.4) 7B.65020 (3.8)	Modified Lucas ignition coil with push-on terminals. Also, a 110-volt cylinder block heater became standard on cars destined for Canada.
			Engines 7B.10454 (3.4) 7B.65030 (3.8)	Improved crankshaft front oil seal (Part No C.24611/1).
			Gearbox JBN.10661	Modified clutch release bearing, with a thicker carbon thrust ring.
August 1968				Ribbed engine cam covers introduced on all engines, replacing the smooth finished alloy type.
December 1968		1B.26356 1B.80406		Cars destined for Austria had standard European LHD headlight units instead of the special type previously fitted.
				All engines fitted with sintered valve seat inserts of a reduced depth (Part Nos C,28224 inlet, and C.28225 exhaust).
			Engine 7B.10995 (3.4)	Non-hydrostatic clutch slave cylinder fitted.
March 1969				All Laycock overdrive units now had a tapered expansion plug in the rear face of the gearbox.

420 and Sovereign production changes

For a key to chassis and engine number sequences, please see the preceding section on Numbers Built and Identification.

Date	RHD change point	LHD change point	Other change point	Change
March 1967	1F.1384	1F.25197		Coupling flange and pinch bolt on the lower steering column of cars with PAS fitted at 90 instead of 45 degrees. The same change later affected cars with unassisted steering, from 1F.1558 (RHD) and 1F.25349 (LHD).
			Engine 7F.2478	Oil seals added to the inlet valve guides.
			Engine 7F.4467	Plain washers replaced lock washers on the main bearing cap bolts, as on all other Jaguar XK engines.
				A 35-amp fuse replaced the 25-amp type for hazard warning light systems on US-market cars.
	1F.2760	1F.26250		Front and rear seat belt anchorage points became standard.
	1F.3401			Final drive ratio on automatic transmission models changed from 3.31:1 to 3.54:1. The same change was later made for LHD cars as well.
	1F.3735	1F.26833		Insulating plate and PVC sleeve fitted to the ammeter to guard against shorting out.
	1F.3858	1F.26849		Painted wire wheels with a forged centre hub and straight spokes made available.
	1F.4093	1F.26908		PAS pump modified, affecting the shaft and pulley mounting and the jockey pulley mounting bracket.
	1F.4332	1F.26992		Powr-Lok limited slip differential option discontinued.
January 1968	1F.5180	1F.27053		Grease nipples added to the rear half-shafts, replacing the sealed for life type.
	1F.5208	1F.27056		Handbrake lever modified to reduce effort.
	1F.5382	1F.27057		Removable element replaced filter gauze in the petrol feed line filter.
			Engine 7F.5997	Improved crankshaft damper plate, with all elements in a single assembly.
July 1968		1F.27280		Headlights on cars destined for Germany included integral side lights. Standard side lights retained but not wired in.
	1F.6629	1F.27389		Modified Lucas ignition coil with push-on terminals.
			Engine 7F.8804	Cars destined for Canada now with 110-volt cylinder block heater as standard.
	1F.6921	1F.27455		Self-adhesive label added to air cleaner end plate above the dipstick to remind owners to fill automatic transmissions with the correct type of oil.
			Engine 7F.8770	Improved crankshaft front oil seal (Part No C.24611/1).
			Engine 7F.8804	Hepworth-Grandage solid-skirt pistons become alternative to Brico split-skirt type.
			Gearbox JBN.10661	Modified clutch release bearing, with a thicker carbon thrust ring.
				Thief-proof domed nuts replaced the knurled brass fixings on the clock.
August 1968				Ribbed type cam covers replaced the smooth alloy type.
December 1968	1F.7100	1F.27491		Ammeter with longer terminal posts to suit extra cabling now fitted.
	1F.8226	1F.27626		Cars with PAS received improved centre tie rod assembly, with steel and neoprene ball end assemblies instead of steel and rubber type.
			Engines	Sintered valve seat inserts of reduced depth (Part Nos C28224 inlet, and C.28225 exhaust).
			Engine 7F.11029	Timing pointer relocated to left-hand side of engine and timing scale relocated to improve accessibility.

145

Date	RHD change point	LHD change point	Other change point	Change
January 1969			Engine 7F.11134	Conrod bolts, nuts and split-pins replaced by bolts and plain nuts with greater tensile strength.
			Engine 7F.11251	Improved clutch with higher rated diaphragm spring, to prevent slip after high mileages.
March 1970				Earlier mercury cell clock no longer available, so a 12-volt type now supplied as a replacement.

SPECIFICATIONS

General Specifications, Jaguar 2.4 & 3.4 (Mk 1)

Engine capacity	2483cc		3442cc	
Bore & Stroke	83 x76.5mm		83 x 106mm	
Compression ratio	8:1 (7:1 optional)		8:1 (7:1 & 9:1 optional)	
Maximum power	112bhp @ 5750rpm		210bhp @ 5500rpm	
Maximum torque	140lb/ft @ 2000rpm		216lb/ft @ 3000rpm	
Carburettors	2 x Solex 24mm downdraught		2 x SU 1.75 HD6	
Transmission	4-speed Moss manual,Overdrive optional			
	3-speed Borg Warner automatic			
Gear ratios	manual	auto	manual	auto
1st	15.35:1		11.95:1	
Low		21.2 to 9.86		17.6 to 7.08
2nd	9.01		6.584	
Intermediate		13.2 to 6.14		10.95 to 8.16
3rd	6.22		4.541	
Top		4.27		3.54
4th	4.55		3.54	
Axle ratios				
Manual/Automatic	4.27:1		3.54:1	
Overdrive	4.55:1		3.77:1	
Clutch	Borg & Beck single dry plate			
Steering	Burman recirculating ball worm and nut			
Brakes	Lockheed Brakemaster hydraulic drums, vacuum assisted			
Suspension				
Front	Independent semi-trailing double wishbones, coil springs and anti-roll bar			
Rear	Cantilevered live axle, parallel radius arms, Panhard rod, half elliptic leaf springs			
Steering wheel	Bluemels 4-spoke			
Turning circle	33ft 6in			
Wheels	4.5J x 15in bolt-on pressed steel (60-spoke wire wheels later optional)			
Tyres	6.40 x 15 Dunlop Road Speed			
Overall length	15ft 0.75in			
Overall width	5ft 6.75in			
Overall height	4ft 9.5in			
Wheelbase	8ft 11.375in			
Track, front	4ft 6.625in			
Track, rear	4ft 2.125in			
Weight	25cwt		27cwt	

Performance

Top speed	101.5mph	120mph
0 to 30mph	4.6 seconds	3.1 seconds
0 to 40mph	6.9 seconds	4.9 seconds
0 to 50mph	11 seconds	7 seconds
0 to 60mph	14.4 seconds	9.1 seconds
0 to 70mph	19.9 seconds	12.4 seconds
0 to 80mph	28.6 seconds	16 seconds
0 to 90mph	39.1 seconds	20.5 seconds
Standing Qtr Mile	24.6 seconds	17.2 seconds
Average fuel consumption	18.3mpg	19.2mpg

General Specifications, Jaguar 2.4 and 3.4 Mk 2

Engine capacity	2483cc	3442cc
Bore & Stroke	83 x76.5mm	83 x 106mm
Compression ratio	8:1 (7:1 optional)	8:1 (7:1 & 9:1 optional)
Maximum power	112bhp @ 5750rpm	210bhp @ 5500rpm
Maximum torque	144lb/ft @ 2000rpm	216lb/ft @ 3000rpm
Carburettors	2 x Solex 24mm downdraught	2 x SU 1.75 HD6
Transmission	4-speed Moss manual,Overdrive optional 3-speed Borg Warner automatic	

Gear ratios	manual (non-OD)	auto	manual (non-OD)	auto
1st	14.42:1		11.95:1	
Low		21.2 to 9.86		17.6 to 7.08
2nd	7.94		6.584	
Intermediate		13.2 to 6.14		10.95 to 8.16
3rd	5.48		4.541	
Top		4.27		3.54
4th	4.27		3.54	

Axle ratios		
Manual/automatic	4.27:1	3.54:1
Overdrive	4.55:1	3.77:1
Clutch	Borg & Beck single dry plate	
Steering	Burman recirculating ball worm and nut	
Brakes	Dunlop discs, 11in front and 11.375in rear, vacuum assisted	
Suspension		
Front	Independent semi-trailing double wishbones, coil springs and anti-roll bar	
Rear	Cantilevered live axle, parallel radius arms, Panhard rod, half elliptic leaf springs	
Steering wheel	2-spoke with half horn ring	
Turning circle	33ft 6in	
Wheels	4.5J (early) then 5J x 15in bolt-on pressed steel (wire wheels optional)	
Tyres	6.40 x 15 Dunlop Road Speed	
Dimensions		
Overall length	15ft 0.75in	
Overall width	5ft 6.75in	
Overall height	4ft 9.75in	
Wheelbase	8ft 11.375in	
Track, front	4ft 7in	
Track, rear	4ft 5.37in	
Weight	26.5cwt	27.5cwt

Performance

Top speed	96.5mph	120mph
0 to 30mph	5.7 seconds	4.5 seconds
0 to 40mph	8.5 seconds	6.4 seconds
0 to 50mph	12.7 seconds	9 seconds
0 to 60mph	17.3 seconds	11.9 seconds
0 to 70mph	23.8 seconds	15.3 seconds
0 to 80mph	33.3 seconds	20 seconds
0 to 90mph	49.9 seconds	26 seconds
Standing Qtr Mile	20.8 seconds	19.1 seconds
Average fuel consumption	19.2mpg	16mpg

General Specifications, Jaguar 3.8 Mk 2

Engine capacity	3781cc
Bore & Stroke	87 x 106mm
Compression ratio	8:1 (7:1 & 9:1 optional)
Maximum power	220bhp @ 5500rpm
Maximum torque	240lb/ft @ 3000rpm
Carburettors	2 x SU 1.75 HD6
Transmission	4-speed Moss manual, Overdrive optional 3-speed Borg Warner automatic
Clutch	Borg & Beck single dry plate
Axle ratios	
Manual/automatic	3.54:1
Overdrive	3.77:1
Gear ratios	As for 3.4 litre Mk 2
Steering	Burman recirculating ball worm and nut
Brakes	Dunlop discs, 11in front and 11.375in rear, vacuum assisted
Suspension	
Front	Independent semi-trailing double wishbones, coil springs and anti-roll bar
Rear	Cantilevered live axle, parallel radius arms, Panhard rod, half elliptic leaf springs
Steering wheel	2-spoke with half horn ring
Turning circle	33ft 6in
Wheels	4.5J (early) then 5J x 15in bolt-on pressed steel (wire wheels optional)
Tyres	6.40 x 15 Dunlop Road Speed
Dimensions	
Overall length	15ft 0.75in
Overall width	5ft 6.75in
Overall height	4ft 9.75in
Wheelbase	8ft 11.375in
Track, front	4ft 7in
Track, rear	4ft 5.37in
Weight	27.5cwt

Performance

Top speed	125mph
0 to 30mph	3.2 seconds
0 to 40mph	4.9 seconds
0 to 50mph	6.4 seconds
0 to 60mph	8.5 seconds
0 to 70mph	11.7 seconds
0 to 80mph	14.6 seconds
0 to 90mph	18.2 seconds
Standing Qtr Mile	16.3 seconds
Average fuel consumption	15.7mpg

General Specifications, Jaguar 240 and 340

Engine capacity	2483cc		3442cc	
Bore & Stroke	83 x 76.5mm		83 x 106mm	
Compression ratio	8:1 (7:1 optional)		8:1 (7:1 & 9:1 optional)	
Maximum power	133bhp @ 5500rpm		210bhp @ 5500rpm	
Maximum torque	146lb/ft @ 3700rpm		216lb/ft @ 3000rpm	
Carburettors	2 x SU 1.75 HS6		2 x SU 1.75 HD6	
Transmission	4-speed Moss manual,Overdrive optional			
	3-speed Borg Warner automatic			
Gear ratios	manual (non-OD)	auto	manual (non-OD)	auto
1st	14.42:1		11.95:1	
Low		21.2 to 9.86		17.6 to 7.08
2nd	7.94		6.584	
Intermediate		13.2 to 6.14		10.95 to 8.16
3rd	5.48		4.541	
Top		4.27		3.54
4th	4.27		3.54	
Axle ratios				
Manual/automatic	4.27:1		3.54:1	
Overdrive	4.55:1		3.77:1	
Clutch	Borg & Beck single dry plate			
Steering	Burman recirculating ball worm and nut			
Brakes	Dunlop discs, 11in front and 11.375in rear, vacuum assisted			
Suspension				
Front	Independent semi-trailing double wishbones, coil springs and anti-roll bar			
Rear	Cantilevered live axle, parallel radius arms, Panhard rod, half elliptic leaf springs			
Steering wheel	2-spoke with half horn ring			
Turning circle	33ft 6in			
Wheels	5J x 15in bolt-on pressed steel (wire wheels optional)			
Tyres	6.40 x 15 Dunlop Road Speed			
Dimensions				
Overall length	14ft 11in			
Overall width	5ft 6.75in			
Overall height	4ft 9.75in			
Wheelbase	8ft 11.375in			
Track, front	4ft 7in			
Track, rear	4ft 5.37in			
Weight	26.5cwt		27.5cwt	

Performance

Top speed	106mph	124mph
0 to 30mph	4.1 seconds	3.5 seconds
0 to 40mph	6.3 seconds	
0 to 50mph	9.3 seconds	6.9 seconds
0 to 60mph	12.3 seconds	
0 to 70mph	16.4 seconds	
0 to 80mph	22.8 seconds	16.6 seconds
0 to 90mph	31 seconds	
Standing Qtr Mile	18.7 seconds	17.2 seconds
Average fuel consumption	18.4mpg	17mpg

General Specifications Daimler V8 2½ Litre and V8-250

Engine capacity	2548cc
Bore & Stroke	76.2 x 69.85mm
Compression ratio	8:.2:1
Maximum power	140bhp @ 5800rpm
Maximum torque	185lb/ft @ 3600rpm
Carburettors	2 x SU 1.75 HD6
Transmission	3-speed Borg Warner automatic
	4-speed manual optional
Clutch	Borg & Beck single dry plate
Axle ratios	
Manual/automatic	Early 4.55:1
	1964-on: 4.27:1
Overdrive	4.55:1
Steering	Burman recirculating ball worm and nut
Brakes	Dunlop discs, 11in front and 11.375in rear, vacuum assisted
Suspension	
Front	Independent semi-trailing double wishbones, coil springs and anti-roll bar
Rear	Cantilevered live axle, parallel radius arms, Panhard rod, half elliptic leaf springs
Steering wheel	2-spoke with half horn ring
Turning circle	33ft 6in
Wheels	5J x 15in bolt-on pressed steel (wire wheels optional)
Tyres	6.40 x 15 Dunlop Road Speed
Dimensions	
Overall length	15ft 0.75in
Overall width	5ft 6.75in
Overall height	4ft 9.75in
Wheelbase	8ft 11.375in
Track, front	4ft 7in
Track, rear	4ft 5.37in
Weight	29cwt

Performance

Top speed	112mph
0 to 60mph	13.8 seconds
0 to 80mph	24.6 seconds
Standing Qtr Mile	20.8 seconds
Average fuel consumption	17mpg

General Specifications, Jaguar S-type 3.4 and 3.8

Engine capacity	3442cc	3781cc
Bore & Stroke	83 x 106mm	87 x 106mm
Compression ratio	8:1 (7:1 & 9:1 optional)	8:1 (7:1 & 9:1 optional)
Maximum power	210bhp @ 5500rpm	220bhp @ 5500rpm
Maximum torque	216lb/ft @ 3000rpm	240lb/ft @ 3000rpm
Carburettors	2 x SU 1.75 Hd6	2 x SU 1.75 HD6
Transmission	4-speed Moss manual,Overdrive optional	
	3-speed Borg Warner automatic	
Gear ratios	As for 3.4 litre and 3.8 litre Mk 2	
Axle ratios		
Manual/automatic	3.54:1	
Overdrive	3.77:1	
Clutch	Borg & Beck single dry plate	
Steering	Burman recirculating ball worm and nut	
Brakes	Dunlop discs, 11in front and 11.375in rear, vacuum assisted	
Suspension		
Front	Independent semi-trailing double wishbones, coil springs and anti-roll bar	
Rear	Independent, lower wishbone/upper driveshaft link, radius arms and twin coil springs	
Steering wheel	2-spoke with half horn ring	
Turning circle	33ft 6in	
Wheels	5J x 15in bolt-on pressed steel (wire wheels optional)	
Tyres	6.40 x 15 Dunlop Road Speed	
Dimensions		
Overall length	15ft 7in	
Overall width	5ft 6.25in	
Overall height	4ft 7.75in	
Wheelbase	8ft 115in	
Track, front	4ft 7.25in	
Track, rear	4ft 6.25in	
Weight	30.7cwt	

Performance

Top speed	119mph	121mph
0 to 30mph	4.1 seconds	3.6 seconds
0 to 40mph	7 seconds	5.5 seconds
0 to 50mph	9.6 seconds	7.5 seconds
0 to 60mph	13.9 seconds	10.2 seconds
0 to 70mph	18.4 seconds	13.3 seconds
0 to 80mph	25.0 seconds	17.1 seconds
0 to 90mph	35.3 seconds	23.5 seconds
Standing Qtr Mile	19.2 seconds	17.1 seconds
Average fuel consumption	19mpg	15mpg

General Specifications, Jaguar 420 and Daimler Sovereign

Engine capacity	4235cc	
Bore & Stroke	92.07 x 106mm	
Compression ratio	8:1 (7:1 & 9:1 optional)	
Maximum power	245bhp @ 5500rpm	
Maximum torque	283lb/ft @ 3750rpm	
Carburettors	2 x SU 2in HD6	
Transmission	4-speed Moss manual, Overdrive optional	
	3-speed Borg Warner automatic	
Clutch	Borg & Beck single dry plate	
Axle ratios		
Manual/automatic	3.31:1 (3.54 aft October 1967)	
Overdrive	3.77:1	
Gear ratios	Manual	Automatic
	11.46	4.80 to 2.40
	7.44	2.92 to 1.46
	5.00	2.0 to 1.0
	3.77	
Overdrive	2.95	
Steering	Burman recirculating ball Varamatic PAS option	
Brakes	Girling discs, 11in front and 11.375in rear, vacuum assisted	
Suspension		
Front	Independent semi-trailing double wishbones, coil springs and anti-roll bar	
Rear	Independent, lower wishbone/upper driveshaft link, radius arms and twin coil springs	
Steering wheel	2-spoke with half horn ring	
Turning circle	33ft 6in	
Wheels	5J x 15in bolt-on pressed steel (wire wheels optional)	
Tyres	6.40 x 15 Dunlop Road Speed	
Dimensions		
Overall length	15ft 0.75in	
Overall width	5ft 7in	
Overall height	4ft 8.25in	
Wheelbase	8ft 11.75in	
Track, front	4ft 7.5in	
Track, rear	4ft 6.5in	
Weight	31cwt	

Performance

Top speed	123mph
0 to 30mph	3.1 seconds
0 to 40mph	5.2 seconds
0 to 50mph	7.0 seconds
0 to 60mph	9.9 seconds
0 to 70mph	12.6 seconds
0 to 80mph	16.7 seconds
0 to 90mph	21.3 seconds
Standing Qtr Mile	16.7 seconds
Average fuel consumption	15.7mpg